Resurrect the Listening Heart and Mind

A Testament from Charmie Gilcrease, the beautiful Kriyaban who themed the two volumes of quotes.

Here is a quote from Yogacharya David that especially speaks to my heart right now. Although this quote isn't from me, it is me.

"Though I made uncountable mistakes, somehow God and Guru never let go of me, though I let go of them. Due to this grace, I learned, changed, and became something new; yet it is a state of consciousness that is deeply familiar—as if it has always been true, always been me. My old life is now seen as something long ago; it is as if I have lived many lives in this one lifespan, some of them almost unrecognizable as being me."

ABOUT YOGACHARYA DAVID

"What can I say about David? I met him when I was 19 and very new on the path this life. He was a long-haired 'hippy' type and rather acerbic in speech. He intrigued and puzzled me. With Mother, I was so in awe I could barely speak around her and could only see the great shining God Self within her. With David, I was able to perceive the human self become the God Self and that experience was a guiding star. Knowing that I, myself, could become my God Self wasn't impossible—hard, but not impossible. Yogacharya David set a wonderful example for many of us."

—CHARMIE GILCREASE

Resurrect the
Listening Heart and Mind
Quotes: Volume One

Yogacharya David R. Hickenbottom

Editor: Ruth M. Lamb, Ph.D

The Cross and The Lotus Publishing
Camano Island, Washington, USA

ISBN: 978-1-957811-16-1 (softcover)
ISBN: 978-1-957811-17-8 (eBook)

All photos courtesy of Carla Hickenbottom Portfolio

Edited by Ruth Lamb

Book design by Jan Westendorp, katodesignandphoto.com

Cover design by Rob Landers, Ruth Lamb, and Jan Westendorp

Printed and bound in Canada by Digital Direct Printing, Victoria, BC

Published by
The Cross and The Lotus Publishing
Camano Island, Washington, USA
Website: www.crossandlotus.com

Contents

Preface

Yogacharya David (1954–2019), a western man who sought to discover the sacred that lies behind the five senses and materialism, was drawn to his Guru, Mother Hamilton in 1974 and his life underwent an evolutionary change. He discovered the grandeur and challenges presented when seeking the highest, most loving Truth: Truth that is within, behind, in front, beneath, and above our daily existence.

Seeking the highest truth consciousness, Yogacharya David discovered his Self, or soul—his unique sovereign integral connection with the Divine Source or Spirit. After many years of dedicated outer and inner work that purifies and attunes the physical, emotional, spiritual, and etheric bodies, he achieved self-realization: an inner connection with Divine Grace as it lives through his unique presence on this beautiful planet.

Through the years, Yogacharya David gave over 1000 talks to devotees, wrote in journals, composed poems, and developed a series of discourses as well as many other writings.

His teachings are now being presented in books. An outline of those published to date is at the end of this book.

Resurrect the Listening Heart and Mind: Quotes Volume One and *Seek the Sacred Code of the Universe: Quotes Volume Two* consist of quotes selected from Yogacharya David's six volume discourse series written between

2013 and 2019. In *Quotes Volume One*, four macro themes: Connection, Joy, Thy Name is Sweet, and Who is our Self? are complemented with fifteen micro themes all designed to bring us closer to our true Self.

Short and replete with wisdom: each discourse is a gem. The quotes chosen here are but a small selection designed to provide upliftment in the moment—a quick reference to start or end a day, or to be a guide during reflective or arduous moments. Significantly, if you receive the words with your heart, you will be able to receive the higher consciousness through the frequency of Yogacharya David's words.

Enjoy.

OM TAT SAT AUM

Introduction

O Infinite Presence
So lost do souls become
From Your comforting solace
Lost in woods of confusion

How is it
That You are so close
So near to heart and breath
With the openness of a child,
That those who are bewildered
Fallen so low
Confused with confusion
Feel forlorn and far from You?

When one knows You
You are the nearest of Friends
The innermost thought
The Life of all Life.[1]

---

1   Yogacharya David, *Climbing the Sacred Mountain: Poems and Prayers of a Western Yogi* (p. 119).

RESURRECT THE LISTENING HEART AND MIND

Yogacharya David climbing in the mountains, 1989.

Connection

GRACE

When in direct relationship with God, giver and receiver merge and are ultimately consumed, one into another. One becomes two, and two become One, a play of Spirit, not to create separation, but to enjoy the giving and receiving in its unending variations.

Think what a dismal life of playing it alone results in when compared to the wonder and beauty of being God's expression and beloved. God, being the senior partner, is not unmindful of the wishes of His beloved; however, His will is far-reaching, wise beyond counting, and takes into account the good of all. Therefore, God is not going to cater to every wish of His beloved, but definitely compensates for every lash that may be received for His Name's sake.

There are places upon the earth that are naturally attuned to more refined spiritual forces. An area, or a cave, can also become spiritually charged due to the influence of a highly advanced soul. The two can work together, when a naturally charged area is frequented by a highly developed being, an ultimate combination of nature and nurture refines the spiritual force.

The Great master Jesus said, "Blessed are they that mourn, for they shall be comforted" (Matthew 5:4). Blessed are they that mourn—the reason you mourn is that you love, and love is the greatest gift of all. Love can be painful when you feel loss, but the master says you shall be comforted. However, not all who mourn feel comfort. That is because in your loss you feel separated and bereft. But there is a greater truth than isolation, a more profound way of being in this world and that is remembering that you are forever connected with God, and by turning your mind towards Him, that blessed Spirit comes into you, and you into Him. This Holy Spirit comforts you, assuages the pain, and makes you know you are never alone.

Jesus said, "Many are called, few are chosen" (Matthew 22:24); and Krishna said, "Of many thousands, one here and there seek Him out, and of those, a rare one rises up to know Him truly as He is" (Gita 7:3, adapted): the path of realization is indeed inscrutable.

Oh Lord, you see to it that the highest good of all be fulfilled. You are the miraculous, healing power that regenerates a cut into repaired skin, brain damage into renewed wholeness, a weakened heart becoming a vigorous pump once again; so many conditions. You are the sole source of healing in little things and large. You are the immense power that explodes as this universe; You are the regenerative ability for rapid, complete, and most perfect healing. You make what many call miracles without a pause or difficulty.

Oh, my most beloved One, miracles abound all about us every day when the sun rises and in the blush of an unfolding flower—exercise Your ability to bring about healing for those who suffer, comfort for those in need, and most of all, Your supreme bliss for Your awakened souls who desire You above all other things. We pray in the name of Your Infinite Self, the masters Jesus and Babaji, Lahiri Mahasaya, Sri Yukteswarji, Master, Mother, and realized masters and saints around this world who You use to carry out Your will here on earth. Be it so—Aum Amen. (At Brother Andre's Basilica in Montreal, Canada.)[2][3]

To be aware of the loving Hand that controls and guides all events in creation, breathes new life into you, makes you young again. And, as Master points out, mind controls the atoms of the body. With the mind merged in the Infinite, then the healing salve of health, youthfulness, and inner knowing that all is well must be in residence, for body, mind, and soul.

With time, close spiritual connections are created—bonds of hearts and souls. Even though God has taken me on this wanderer's life for now, I feel that powerful

---

2   Unless otherwise denoted, "Mother" stands for Mother Hamilton.

3   Unless otherwise denoted, "Master" stands for Paramhansa Yogananda.

connection in God with you, even as I felt it with Mother. Time, space, age, circumstances in life, all this fades into a muted background, and what stands crystal clear is my union with God, and with all dear friends.

Sri Yukteswarji said in his *Holy Science* that God fulfills all of the heart's desires. I can attest to this truth.

In the fullness of this heart, overflowing with the Divine Presence, I write these words: From this heart may that same love, power, and light flood out over all time and space, and touch your heart and soul—may you feel the same greatness and timelessness of Spirit in our Infinite Beloved that I feel now.

───※───

The true aspirant knows that what produces real, lasting happiness is communion with God, the Self, united with the infinite Being, is eternal and is filled with supreme Consciousness and Bliss.

───※───

As an aspirant for truth and realization you either qualify or disqualify yourself, based on the purity of your yearning for God. Grace can give you an experience in upliftment, peace, bliss, joy, or some tremendous realization, but this is only the beginning of your journey.

───※───

To make continuous progress, you must ever apply the methods a qualified preceptor gives to you. Without this application, the source of Grace will be dammed up, and the flow of spiritual *living waters* will dry up. Without the flow of these living waters, aspiration will evaporate for without Grace, no real progress can be made.

———∞———

What I find truly awe-inspiring is how He takes care of us with unfailing love and attention to detail. Some may call it coincidence or lucky breaks, but when time after time His total inner direction and outer answers to our needs are miraculously fulfilled, one must finally come to the conclusion that luck or coincidence simply does not suffice to explain how He perfectly takes care of us.

———∞———

I see the ways that many limit themselves in their growth of consciousness. But I know that the seed of yearning will not be denied, and though the outer shell of the seed may resist the power of growth, soon the limiting shell will burst wide open as tender shoots reach out to the light.

———∞———

Impossible tasks seem to be ahead of me, things to be accomplished before I am to leave this body. However, what seems to be impossible to me is easily accomplished by an all-powerful God. When I survey what needs to be done, it looks to be an unconquerable mountain. But that is just me, my localized view. I would be a fool to rely on my own resources as a human being.

———∞———

Take heart, you are not left helpless against an onslaught of materialism; rather, you have the means to connect with God in all circumstances and thus build a bridge to the Infinite.

———— ∞ ————

Living a life of service carries with it built-in Grace; we feel unburdened through our right attitude. Now love and joy glow at the heart of our service and we are sustained by an all-pervading power. In perfect service, we discover one of the great secrets of living a truly successful life.

———— ∞ ————

I feel the great Spirit in me in touch with you. Love is the hallmark of this Spirit, the love that is God—a love that knows no bounds.

———— ∞ ————

The direction Grace goes can be interactive: we may direct that power through our intention, such as when we pray for another, or the inner power will also direct us, as when virtue goes out of us spontaneously.

———— ∞ ————

Feel the waves of joy in accomplishment, we may feel sorrow at a loss, but being anchored in the Divine, we never lose connection with who and what we truly are.

———— ∞ ————

May your own travels in life toward enlightenment be rapid and every obstacle be overcome in the face of your enduring persistence and God's grace.

———∽∞∽———

I earnestly wish you peace, an inner assurance that God is with you and guiding you, and that you feel the warmth and love of association that God effortlessly connects us all, wherever we may be, anywhere around this globe, or beyond.

———∽∞∽———

To break out of the earth's gravity, a rocket must attain the speed of 25,000 miles per hour. To break the gravity of earthly attachment, we must necessarily travel at the speed of God! which can only be attained by His booster rocket of Grace.

We draw Grace to ourselves when we love the Lord God with all our heart, mind, strength, and soul. To attain the velocity we need by finding that part of God, we must have the desire for God beyond all other desires. Then, He cannot stay away, but will be drawn irresistibly by the magnet of our love—we then break free of earthly bonds and float free in His truth and His bliss.

———∽∞∽———

The very root of this universe is Ananda; it is an explosion of joyful-bliss. And life, when lived in God, is filled with Divine Presence. No matter how far we wander from our

Source, it never stops being the essence of who and what we are; this is a fact. It has been a source of great mischief that religious leaders invented eternal hell and damnation.

Reason tells us that God, being the creator of all and who is more loving than the most devoted parent, will never abandon His children, never! We are made in His likeness and His image. Therefore, we are eternally His.

———⊗⊗⊗———

It was ignorance and arrogance that made religious institutions square off against science, and, as perhaps was predictable, science then polarized itself against religion. In fact, both are explorers and seekers of truth; both should be joined in discovering physical and metaphysical realms.

No matter the factual gains of science, there will always be a mystery to this creation. On one level of experience, matter, like Spirit, will defy knowing from whence things come and whither they go.

———⊗⊗⊗———

All of what I have in God is yours, for I send out all that He gives me without reservation. May all be well, my dear ones, and most of all, may you ever be filled with the Divine Presence deep within your heart and soul.

———⊗⊗⊗———

I am always happy to have Him working through me, according to what He chooses—for God and Gurus' will is always uppermost in my life. While they are in charge, I know that everything happens according the highest good of all concerned; for that is the nature of God's will—it is, by definition, for the utmost benevolence. Therefore, we are always connected through that highest good, and the work that God does here is also done in you, for in Him there is no separation.

—∞—

What is perhaps the strongest bond in a marriage and represents the greatest potential, is the spiritual bond that goes beyond personality, situation, or worldly pressures. One key is a mutual understanding that God has brought you together, faith that you are meant to be a couple, and by remaining spiritually aligned, God can work out the kinks and make things even better between you; knowing that your attunement with God brings out more love, tolerance, patience, and the ability to see the divinity in one another—what greater intimacy is there than that!

When a couple seeks to serve God in one another, there are no limits to the fulfillment that can come about as a result.

—∞—

Husband and wife who through time and experience, deepen their relationship and spiritual attunement, can successfully transmute all experiences into spiritual awareness. Through divine prompting, there may be physical union that plays a part in their lives which elevates the sexual experience into spiritual union. The after-effect is merging into an ocean of Infinite expanse. On a human level, there will always be differences between two people, but in Spirit, there is a perfect joining of two souls into One.

———⊗⊗⊗———

Great principles prove themselves to be timeless. We collectively suffer when true principles are trampled, we are all affected when any one of our sisters or brothers are treated with disrespect—their inner qualities not seen or even looked for.

———⊗⊗⊗———

At the end of the day, you want to feel that you are in right relationship with God and Gurus—that you may stand easy and breathe the fresh air of openness and truth.

———⊗⊗⊗———

Individuals can cultivate a desire to be a good and faithful servant of God, but it is only Grace being born in the world of the individual that spiritual realization can really come into its own. An inner light is calling to awaken the shepherds—something special is coming; the fulfillment of a promise made at the foundation of creation—birth of a God-man, a God-woman!

———⊗⊗⊗———

May Master ever bless you and his grace lift you constantly higher into the supreme divine consciousness of his infinite Beloved.

———⊗⊗⊗———

Having become established in eternal Life, a true master's grace can communicate itself to a sincere devotee throughout all time and without regard for spatial distance. The electricity of their grace is ever flowing to us; in fact, it is all around us, but only if we plug in, and have the capacity of utilizing that flow of spiritual power, can it really make a difference in our lives.

———

In a world that divides humanity into those who are chosen and others who are outsiders, the Creator recognizes no such barriers. Those who love, and act on that love, are His proclaimed brothers and sisters.

———

In dealings with customers, do you employ the Golden Rule: Treat your customers as you would want to be treated? The way you work with co-workers, employees, and bosses—do you treat all others the way you would want to be treated if you were in their position? The very best owners, managers, and employees do exactly this.

These Golden Rule types are the kind of people you want to work for. They are the kind of workers you want in your business, and companies, and with this motto branded into their thinking, words, and actions, these are the kind of businesses you want to patronize.

———

For those who perceive the one true Creator behind all religious impulses the world over, then, as Mother

Hamilton stated, there is only one God and one reli-gion—a religion beyond secular divisions.

There is only one supreme truth—and all the various religions are but descriptions of our human relation-ship with that truth, or God. In the end, all religions are expressions of the same desire to know God.

———— ∞ ————

Entering into the silence of God-consciousness, we are perfectly content, and this awareness loops us back into even greater stillness—we no longer have need of our constant, restless, nature, and it simply drops away. So, let us begin, now.

———— ∞ ————

We celebrate fathers, for the vital role you play in the human drama of family. Indeed, when fathers are absent, families and communities suffer, so you are an essential part of both family and community.

———— ∞ ————

God creates through you, and as a result, you maintain your connection with God, even while living in a physical body. In this way, the spiritual scientist proves through practical experience that one may be on intimate terms with the creation, and be One with God.

———— ∞ ————

What glory there is in divine communion, not only with our Heavenly Father/Divine Mother but also with all brothers and sisters coming together in spirit. This superior union in Spirit connects us all and is greater than bonds of blood, greater than friendships based on common worldly interests, for it goes to the innermost core of the Atman or Soul—our part of God.

———

Spiritual Relationship is geared toward mutual advancement in God-awareness. Other relationships can also be important, but they cannot match the highest common good that is derived from communion through infinite Spirit.

———

Let there be civility, kindness, a desire to understand another's point of view—a desire to find the common ground of universal kinship upon which to build lasting relationships with all men and women. Hate and intolerance are not a solution—only mutual respect and love heal.

———

When giving thanks, you feel a loving relationship with God. It is grace that is coming into your body: giving it all that is needed for healing, providing prosperity as it flows to you in unknown and delightful ways, that relationships are being healed in you and in others—it all comes from the exhaustless storehouse of He who creates vast universes.

While His Presence is beyond the scope of the puny

little human mind to encompass, He also comes in personal, loving, and tender ways to each person, and all parts of His creation.

⎯⎯⎯

When in need of healing, God may heal you directly through grace, He may also send to you the right people or circumstances to enact healing, or He may give you strength and perspective to endure what must be gone through. And this is true for prosperity and broken relationships as well. It is also the way in which you achieve God-realization.

⎯⎯⎯

I give You thanks, not because You require it, but because it puts me in right relationship with You, because it helps open the inner floodgates of Your power, intelligence, and love. You create all that is and all that is to come, and for what You give, I offer You my most humble and loving gratitude.

⎯⎯⎯

As I look back, it has been a life of discipleship now for many years. Decades of powerful forces that Mother unleashed in this form, many years of His power and glory intermingling their influence into my life—governing and shepherding, and gradually transforming the body, mind, and soul into a living manifestation of His Light.

It has been years of testing, as oppositional forces of desire nature, fear, and obstinance fought for control of

this form. Though I made uncountable mistakes, somehow God and Guru never let go of me, though I let go of
them. Due to this grace, I learned, changed, and became
something new, yet it is a state of consciousness that is
deeply familiar—as if it has always been true, always been
me. My old life is now seen as something long ago—it is
as if I have lived many lives in this one lifespan, some of
them almost unrecognizable as being me.

———

You are continually being blessed. As Master once said,
"You have God's blessings, you have Gurus blessings, all
that is required now are your blessings!"

———

There are those who do not think they have the time
or the interest to know God. But that is only because
they have not been properly introduced. To know God is
to love Him, and to love Him is to know Him in greater
measure.

———

Communion in God makes a bond of one with one
another; not simply through personal psychic connection,
but through the purity of God-experience.

———

Become an active receiver, go within and commune with
our Infinite Beloved, and through Him, with all.

———

It is the greatest joy that we may go to God together. He blesses us so that each of us fulfills the tasks He has given. In saying this as my birthday wish, I do not blow out the lit candle, but ask that lighted souls everywhere may manifest more and more light for the One, and for all. (Yogacharya David's birthday is February 26.)

Surely, we are all in His hands, each and every moment of the day.

When pain comes, it is turned over to God, and we are given the ability to endure it or rise above it. Our best Friend is always with us, and this is a wonderful comfort.

Inner attunement to spiritual grace greatly speeds up healing.

Affirm that I am made in the likeness and image of perfect Divine Consciousness; all things are possible and doable through Grace.

God chooses the moment in time to reveal Himself: He plants the mustard seed that grows into a prodigious tree of realization where the birds of Heaven may find branches of realization to perch upon.

Through deeper meditation, the aspirant achieves true God-contact; a knowing connection grows and convinces the devotee down to the cellular level that God is within him or her. When the power of God passes through that devotee, then healing of the body, mind, and spirit occurs; also, courage, clarity of mind, and purpose, and joyful bliss can be transmitted.

With a clear connection to God, mountainous obstacles are removed—and if God wills it, physical mountains tumble down as well.

BAPTISM

Our simple love and faith form a bond with God that cannot be broken, and while it is true that all souls have God with them, it is only His awakened ones who are conscious of this omniscient Presence—and this makes all the difference.

⸎

This morning, I sit watching the sun slowly lighten darkness into a rosy aura. The Aum sings its song of many notes, the eyes close and bliss plays along the spine. The thought of the Silken Road arises in the mind to describe the smooth flow of bliss in the spine and brain. The desire to share this with one and with all wells up inside me; to describe in order to awaken, to think upon others in order to convey this experience, to collapse time and space so that no barriers exist between I and Thou and His blessed children.

The curse of leaving the Garden of God is lifted, the redemption of the Soul is at hand, baptized in Living Waters, and barren no more—a prayer spontaneously erupts in my mind as a picture of Living Waters flowing into, and uplifting, all creation into native Spirit—separation but a dream once dreamed long ago.

⸎

The one gift God gives daily and that I treasure first and foremost is His Presence—which is a constant in my life. This Presence fills my heart to overflowing to such a degree that it spontaneously flows out to you—there is no greater gift than this—it is never ending, never slackening, always increasing, and bursting the banks of every limitation.

Oh, what Bliss is mine! And all I wish to do is spend my life in awakening this same gift in you, and in all.

This morning, on the day of a full moon and Good Friday, God has shown me the connection between Cain and Abel and the two thieves on the cross. How good God is, how sublime and perfect are the teachings in these stories.

These stories are ostensibly about history dating back thousands of years, but even more meaningfully, these stories are descriptions of the son of man nature and the Son of God nature residing in every man and woman the world over.

It is the story of the redemption of every individual who would seek out Christ Consciousness, by whatever name it may be called. It is the story of you and me.

The path to enlightenment will strip you of everything you know and what you think you know. This empties the cup of the human mind so that you may be born anew in Spirit.

When you find that doubt enshrouds you, remember that faith, loyalty, and perseverance are your allies— they will see you through any dark night the soul may encounter. Having traversed this transit of shadows and demons, you will once again merge into light, expansiveness, and a knowing oneness with your beloved Creator—you will once again be your true Self.

——⦿——

Losing fear of pain, seeing the underlying life-force as coming from God behind the pain signals, and then feeling God's Presence in the form of bliss has a tremendously palliative effect in suffering. Not only can it ease suffering in itself, it also opens intuition so that the Divine Force may be free to affect a cure.

——⦿——

The Baptism of Fire, hinted at by Jesus, is an internal conflagration of vast proportions. For some, entering the Mystical Crucifixion, this baptism of fire is of relatively short duration. But in certain cases, Divine Will uses this fire to help purify not only His devotee, but for the greater good as well. Therefore, this fire may extend over many years, or even the span of a life in rare cases.

This fire may or may not create heat in the physical body, but it definitely rages through the subtle body. I have lived with this Baptism of Fire for nearly forty years now. In the beginning, the purpose was more to do with this body and the karma associated with it. Then it gradually began to be of help to others, and in this third stage, it has to do with being of service to this world. So, the notion of suffering in eternal fire has a certain ring of familiarity to it for me!

To "receive" Jesus Christ is more than to proclaim faith in his Divinity, it means to realize through experience your same Divinity. It means you have looked within and you have seen the Divine Light shining as a star; you have been inspired by three wisdom kings to surrender the gold of the world, the bitterness of the world, and even your joy, and worship at the feet of the Christ-Light being born within you. It is to protect that Light from the vain jealousy and hatred of King Herod, seething within and seeking to destroy the Light. It is to love and nurture that Christ-Child-Light at every turn, to never deny it, or side with the forces of this world in their desire to suppress that same Light.

To receive the Christ means that you experience the whole story within you.

When our whole being is lit up with the eternal Light, we become a finely decorated tree with the spine as the trunk and nerves the branches. The Star of the East is seen at the Christ Center of the ajna, and gifts are delivered when those fine spiritual feelings are felt throughout our being. Christ is born anytime the Presence of God is felt and there are acts of loving service.

It is also entirely fitting to meditate upon the inner drama of God born in the human. While it is true that all humankind has the Christ-seed within, for most of humanity it lies in potential only. For aspiring souls that seed awakens, sending out branches to the Light, roots deep into the Soul. It is the tree of life that is growing right within us! New growth captures new Light, new revelations and ever-new bliss.

—∞—

"Oh Lord, why do You wait even a moment when such a cry comes to You from sincere devotees?" And You answer: "Do you not realize that when my son Jesus said you cannot pour new wine into an old wineskin, he was speaking of this very thing?" For this is the truth—the old wineskin of limited human consciousness, and the new wine of Christ Consciousness, cannot merge until powerful changes come about that makes Divine Consciousness possible in the individual devotee.

What we go through is not without meaning—there is purpose behind everything we are put through—that is especially true when you create a pure intention to seek God alone.

—∞—

This writing is dedicated to all those who follow the Way of the Cross and the Christ. It has been said that one should write with one's own blood, and this I do. For the Way of the Cross demands everything of who you are, everything you wish to be. And what do you receive in return? Everything that is God becomes your own. You walk this path alone. Even as Jesus was stripped of everything, even his dignity as he went the Way of the Cross.

Blessings to all who strive to emulate our beloved Christ in every detail—in his crucifixion and in his resurrection.

———✵———

There are many wonderful things about this world, but none compares to the universal Christ-presence sown throughout creation, and that is most definitely residing deeply in you.

———✵———

First Nations people certainly had their favored sacred places, but there was also the idea that the earth itself is sacred and that animals play a special role in this interplay between spirit, earth, and humans. Those early inhabitants lived close to earth's elements, and many were souls sensitively attuned to this connection, open to the transformative experiences that can come by being in untrammeled nature.

———✵———

We are blessed beyond comprehension through our deepened connection with God-tuned beings—perfected in the fires of testing and blazing with the pure Light of Divine Consciousness.

———✵———

Achieving union with God makes the second stage of the *love of God* a living reality. You are now merged in universal divine love. Love naturally pours through your heart; love guides and enlightens you; it effortlessly flows through every part of your being in thought, word, and action. Divine Love is now part and parcel of your being.

———∽∾∽———

It is only God who is with us from our first breath to our last; it is only God who will be with us on our astral journey in between lives here on earth and for all time.

———∽∾∽———

It has been His sweet will to burn with an inner fire each day in these three bodies—a purification rite of His choosing. Although few would necessarily notice, Carla is often highly attuned to the needs of this body, even before I am. Through her able assistance, I have been kept functioning, and she has kept this body in health when otherwise it may have very well dispersed into vaporized atoms from which it originated.

———∽∾∽———

This Easter morning, it came clear from God that what I was experiencing is part of the Mystical Crucifixion on a wider plane of consciousness—I was in the midst of the two great, grinding, oppositional forces of creation. It is fascinating, it truly is, to be taken through these times and have God as my perfect Guide. I am perfectly sensitive to the fact that there are those who would doubt such experiences; nevertheless, I can tell one and all that I am perfectly sane; I am not given to fanciful imaginations; and I am not extraordinary, but God makes it all possible through this form. It is the most interesting, challenging, and fulfilling life one can possibly live. I feel quite blessed to have God and Gurus as the sole power and guide in my life.

―∞∞―

This path, this journey, is only for those who have complete commitment.

―∞∞―

Confusion and suffering occur when incarnating souls do not remember why they have come. Knowing God and serving Him in all souls in accordance with His inner direction has been, and continues to be, the real purpose of my life.

―∞∞―

The very nerves of the body must be strengthened, or they would be burned out in an instant upon contact with these high frequency energies. However, through repeated exposure to uplifting experiences, the body system gradually changes, making it a divinely fit instrument. The rising expanding energy meets the knot points in the spine and brain—a struggle ensues as physical and psychological obstacles keep the new transforming energy from flowing easily and smoothly. Emotional and psychological kinks must be worked out—these kinks are interlocked with physical blockages—the process of sadhana exposes all past emotional obstructions and false, limiting beliefs.

Meeting and moving through these mental sticking-points gradually purifies the practitioner; for Truth cannot reveal itself when selfishness, greed, fear, and anger loom large. The cup of consciousness must be emptied of all personal attachments—there can be no exceptions.

──⟨∞⟩──

Through deepened meditation and upliftment, a new body in Christ is generated and brought fully into being. The total yearning of heart, mind, and soul is part of this tremendous cleansing and transformation.

──⟨∞⟩──

God's love, His wisdom-thoughts, and His bliss are not for some distant future in our life, but are with us even now, when we are fully open to it.

──⟨∞⟩──

Mother took me on such a tremendous journey, physically demanding, mentally exacting, emotionally expanding—in short, it tested me in every possible way than I could have ever anticipated. From the Mystical Crucifixion of the physical, energetic, and mental, each stage carried with its own tests and its upliftment. Surely, there is no greater challenge and no comparable reward.

──⟨∞⟩──

Mother's first measurement for complete God-realization is the ability to both live in the world of duality and be filled with the bliss of God. This mirrors Sri Yukteswarji's statement that God-realization is ever-new joy—to know within you, "I am living in that blissful-joy, feeling God's Presence, day and night without a break."

It can be tempting to see the suffering of another and wonder why it is so upsetting to him or her or to thank one's lucky stars that it is not your situation. But compassion, the universal vision, makes all lives deeply connected with one's own; therefore, the suffering of another is not simply something to be seen from a distance, but it is a part of us.

To be useful to another experiencing such suffering does not require that we too become identified with the object of suffering, for that would be the blind leading the blind, but for us to remain in our oneness with God while also being conscious of the suffering of another.

Creation came in six stages, and the three days of the crucifixion are also three stages—one representing the physical, another the astral or energetic, and the third, the idea or causal body. We too go through these stages, but one day, one year, or ten years, or more, may be required for each stage to be complete.

So, to get through these stages saints think, "I am sharing this feeling of being crucified with the Christ," or, "I am on the battlefield with Arjuna and Krishna," or, "I am in the night of testing with the Buddha." By putting the mind on a divine personality going through these experiences, there is a link made between the human and the divine that allows grace to enter into the experience. This grace brings strength, even joy, during the anguish and removes the fear and the isolation that so often comes with suffering.

When we know there is meaning behind all our experiences, then we can endure so much more. When we feel that God and Guru have forgotten us, and they do not see our pain or suffering, then we can go down a spiral of despair. When God gives us a tremendous load, the bridge supporting that great weight may creak and groan, but this only indicates the stress of what is being transported, not a lack of faith, as this is exactly what God has asked us to do.

In our deepest soul, we feel that this is what has been given to us; it is His will, and we are privileged to be sharing the load that He must carry on a daily basis. For God is all that is; therefore, He is suffering all the pain that all creation experiences—He feels everything that every person goes through; He knows the reason for which everything occurs, and that it is fulfilling a high purpose.

The nature of living a spiritual life is, in its most simple form, the individual in union with the deepest sense of Self, and then knowing that the same divine Self is present throughout creation.

The guru ignites a fire in the devotee that results in focused sadhana.

—⊶∞⊷—

God and the kingdom of Heaven are to be found within us.

—⊶∞⊷—

To know God, we must experience God.

—⊶∞⊷—

Celestial Support

Feel God smile. Feel fresh spring air blow through you—feel lighter, optimistic, and secure. The thought of Krishna comes to mind, he is smiling even when calamitous events are unfolding. Why is he smiling? Because he sees the Big Picture, not just the little frames of individual incidents. The Big Picture tells him that all is occurring exactly as it ought to, and that all is working for the highest good of all.

———

To enter the room where the master dwells means to enter deeply into your yogi's cave of meditation and deep communion with God.

In a world of suffering and isolation, it comes as a great amazement to find that right within your own consciousness lies a treasure trove of union with the eternal, all blissful Consciousness of God. Without the clarion call of great souls who have themselves discovered this greatest of open secrets, who would guess at this truth?

———

Besides the fall equinox being a time of harvest and thanksgiving, it is also known to bring a special opportunity for focusing on things spiritual. Spring, summer, fall, and winter each have their beginning and end, and each of these yearly cycles correspond to times in the day, early morning, noon, evening, and midnight. Sensitive yogis noticed that these times of the day, and times of the year, present an opening into higher consciousness for the meditator.

—∞∞∞—

By mentally staying connected to God, you remain anchored to your vast, Divine Nature, even while you interact with the pain and disappointment of this world.

It is no accident that the birth of Jesus is marked at the winter time of year. Symbolically, it is the depth of darkness and the beginning of the procession to the light; a perfect time for the birth of the "Light of the world" to incarnate. Historians tell us that for the shepherds to be out tending their flocks at night, as depicted in the scriptures, it would be springtime, lambing season. So, December would not be the historical birth date of Jesus, but March or April. However, not only is the end of December symbolically right, but the intense purification before the solstice, followed by uplifting joy, is the perfect time for the birth of the savior.

When we understand that this increasing intensity is part of a purification rite, and its purpose is the birth of something new, then we can consciously cooperate with this progression, understand it, and receive the greatest benefits from its annual occurrence.

Rejoice, for something wonderful is coming! Prepare the way and spread your wings so that the seasonal uplifting currents will carry you heavenward; listen carefully and you will hear the celestial music of the spheres. The tender birth of the Christ-child is coming; the ancient prophesies are to be fulfilled right within your own being.

The winter solstice occurs on or near December 21st. The solstice marks the shortest day of sunlight due to the earth's tilt and its rotation around the sun. It has long been noted that celestial movements relate to changes in consciousness, and from this observation, astrology had its origins. The winter solstice and its opposite, the summer solstice, as well as the two equinoxes, have special relevance to inner changes as well as the more obvious outer changes.

Sri Yukteswarji spokeof the special significance of the solstice and equinox as times that a tide of cosmic uplift facilitates a transformation of consciousness to the sensitively attuned.

Yogis have marked the Summer Solstice with a special reverence for thousands of years. In our modern way of living, we oftentimes become indifferent to the subtle changes in nature, even immune to the change of seasons. The yogis with highly sensitive nervous systems marked these changes, feeling the powerful but refined shifts of vibration throughout the day, seasons, years, and even millennial flux.

Let us gather in deepened meditation and chanting to avail ourselves of the "thinning" of the veil of separation that occurs during the Solstice. Spiritual skies with a blue vault above and a brilliant Light shining everywhere but

with no center reveals itself and make heavenly consciousness an easy reach. Powerful cosmic rays from Divine
Consciousness easily flow from celestial regions.

—◦◦◦◦—

For millennia, yogis and mystics from every nook and
clime of the world have recognized the subtle, but powerful, effects of different times of the day, the year, and
movements of the zodiacal clock.

One of the principles that yogis discovered is that you
can take full advantage of these recurring zodiac cycles.
For instance, with the Winter Solstice you can deepen
your meditation, spread your wings, so to speak, to take
advantage of these uplifting currents.

And while these active solstice forces may stir up difficult psycho-emotional energies as well, they can then
make this a time for purification, as it is your spiritual
work to pass these subconscious moods into the Light.
It is valuable to be aware of these invisible, but powerful,
forces and use them to your advantage.

—◦◦◦◦—

It is a fascinating idea that we are so strongly connected
with all creation, such that distant constellations of stars
could be influencing us here on earth. We all certainly
feel the effects of lunar cycles. We all know that there are
mysterious rhythms in our lives in which things either go
uncommonly smoothly, or, it seems that we are fighting
invisible currents of opposition all the way. The warp and
woof of these events can be chalked up to chance, but

isn't it possible there are lawfully-governed undercurrents in life that we can sometimes trace, even anticipate?

In our perception of these outer influences, it is important to know that we have a power deep within us that supersedes all outer influences. Whether we come into contact with a negative personality, situation, or contrary stellar influence, we are reminded that the power of God within is greater. This does not mean that we will not have to contend with outer forces, but that we should not give it preeminence in our mind. The light, intelligence, love, and joy of God is superior to creation, and tapping into that internal power is our best weapon for combating negative influences.

Of course, these outer influences are not negative only—there are powerful external forces that help lift us up as well. The proximity of highly developed souls in our life, salubrious situations that support our spiritual aspirations, and the turning of the celestial clock at such times as the Summer Solstice all can bring the positive. Sri Yukteswarji tells us this is a special time. By spreading our meditational wings, we benefit from the powerful upward drafts that are present at this time.

In consciousness there is demonstrably no separation of time or space. Through the all-pervasive Divine Consciousness there is instantaneous and direct connection. Thoughts, feelings, energies, and experiences of others can all be known through God-experience. It is different from a psychic connection, in which a few of the same things may be known. When Divine Consciousness is the medium there is a Supreme Intelligence directing it all, and the Presence of God is constant.

———

I know from my own experience that deepened prayer brings me closer to God and thus acts as a blessing to the one praying. Whether it is an individual, or dozens, hundreds, thousands or millions, prayer has the capacity to bend and re-shape reality in positive ways.

One person, close to God, may have a greater effect than millions, but no prayer is lost or insignificant in the eyes of the Lord.

Let each one of us deepen our communion with the Infinite and therefore be a greater conduit for His blessings going out to this creation.

———

We can drink deeply from the well of Bliss within, and then share that Divine Light with all the world. We have much more to share with this world when we have contacted God first!

———

Let us follow that star by going deeper into a meditative state in which we are illumined within by the Christ Light. Let us hear the angelic music of Spirit singing the song of Bliss and Joy that is within and everywhere about us and manifests as universal love and service.

———

Just as a radio can receive messages from invisible signals, and a transmitter can broadcast the same, so built within a human being a soul may receive and broadcast spiritual consciousness.

———∞———

Watch how the here-and-now God-experience lends a halo of peace and joy to both the past and the future. In this way, the omnipresence of the Infinite glows from every nook and cranny of your mind and life-experience. Now peace, love, and joy are your constant and abiding companions through every moment of every day for your pilgrimage through life!

The meaning of life is found in the evolution of consciousness and its ultimate merging with Divine Consciousness.

———∞———

There are places in nature that have pure, powerful, uplifting currents systemic to their nature. Other places have been the haunts of saints and realized beings that take on their vibration, and that feeling remains. Then there are places that are a combination of both, natural temples that are supported by holy men and women who find it conducive to be in a salubrious environment, and make it even more so through their own uplifted states of minds.

———∞———

To have such a feeling for a place, connecting you with tribe, ancestors, and unity of spirit, is a long step towards experiencing the unifying Spirit that ties individual consciousness to the Supreme Consciousness of Omnipresence and Omniscience.

───※───

While God is known to be equally present everywhere in His creation, He seems to be more "equally present" in some places than others!

───※───

It is in silent reclusiveness that my consciousness effortlessly merges into all-consciousness, and through that to you. For, in touching the fabric of God, one must be connected to all that God is, including His creation.

───※───

What a love-affair God has created. He makes us journey far away from Him in consciousness. Then, He draws us back to Himself; creating magnetism when the time is right that we cannot, and do not want to, resist.

───※───

Seek out those sacred places and receive their blessings, as well as adding your blessings to them from your uplifted state of mind. Some places in Nature are simply spiritually charged; there may be spots where saints and those of high consciousness imbued them with vibrational power, and then there are those spots that have become pilgrimage spots where, over many years, pilgrims have added their consciousness to an already powerful place.

I have felt the regenerational force pulsating all around me in our meandering through woods, sitting at the feet of pounding waterfalls, and peering up stark rocked cliffs covered in green, orange, and red lichen.

There are certainly special places that resonate with powerful spiritual vibrations in nature that are systemic to the area itself.

Whether it is a walk in your garden, a local park, or beside a water shore, or observing a mountain view, or passing beside ancient giants of the forest, seek out the healing currents that run abundantly throughout nature and know the great benefits that God is constantly giving to us through this land that is sacred.

From Jesus and Babaji, to Lahiri Mahasaya, Sri Yuketswarji, Master, and Mother as well as Swami Ramdas, Mother Krishnabai, and Swami Satchidananda, and the multitude of truly worshipful saints and realized beings down through the ages, I give humble thanks for the lives they led, the teachings they generously imparted, and the truly superior example of their lives. They dedicated their lives and their all to the upliftment and enlightenment of this world.

Babaji, Jesus, Lahiri Mahasaya, Sri Yukteswarji, Master, and Mother all stand at the ready to render us the greatest aid on the most tremendous adventure we will ever embark upon. The Mahavatar is naught else but pure God-consciousness, and thus a direct conduit to the Infinite.

———∞———

Paramhansa Yogananda has left his mark for all of us to follow in doing what he did, knowing what he knew, becoming what he became; for he is the archetype for a rapidly-developing consciousness in this world.

———∞———

We have been given a gift beyond measure in having living examples in our guru-lineage and via other saints from around the world. We have been given the very highest methods for realizing God, and we have been shown examples of who and what we should be in God. We need those examples, and along the way, we need encouragement.

———∞———

To the sensitive yogi, Master said that there are four times of transition each day. Of course, we are all familiar with sunrise, sunset, noon, and midnight as common markers of the day. However, the meditating yogi will notice special times of the day that are propitious for going within, 4–6 a.m., 11 a.m.–noon, 5–6 p.m., and 10–midnight. One can take advantage of these subtle but powerful tides of energy by using these times for prayer and meditation.

———✦———

As I look upstream at the successive waterfalls, there is a pool of water with a rocky landing beyond. I thought, Babaji is with me, and his radiant presence manifests on the rocky landing, spreading to the whole scene before me. The air itself scintillates with his vibration; I feel him both near and all around.

———✦———

Almost twenty years ago now, when at Cloud Mountain during a year of silence and solitude, I had several experiences with the great Mahayogi.[4] In one of these, I felt him so close and beseech him to come to me in body. In blunt language, he refuses and made it known to me that I am to realize his universal nature, not limit him to a physical form. Since that time, he has occasionally come to me with his personal "signature," but expansive and universal—as well as in the perfect intimacy of thought transference.

"Oh, beautiful master, you come in this superior form-less-form and your supreme consciousness touches my own—thereby, I am blessed. You teach me non-attachment to form, and thereby free me of local biases, making me know that we are not material stuff, but super-existence that cannot be constrained by a simple body or location. Your very nature is universal, and through the touch of your consciousness, you make me know that I too am of universal nature. Your blessings are purity itself. I bow to you and feel myself dissolved into God's omniscient Self."

---

4   Yogacharya David is referring to Babaji of the Kriya Yoga lineage.

Belief is something of the mind, but faith comes from some place more fundamental to our being. Faith connects the mind, in a viable way, to the supreme power of the Creator and in that connection, the higher power of Grace flows.

It truly is a great thing when you dedicate a space to your practice. It may be a room, a corner of a room, or a closet space you claim. Your practice builds a power in that space, just as it does in the things you use, such as your meditation blanket, beads, and altar. If one day, you feel drained or uninspired, the vibration you have invested into your meditation space will lift you up and support you—helping to transform a tough day into a good one.

Yoga means to yoke ourselves to God, not this world.

In this hand-in-glove relationship, we are at peace, we experience bliss, we know beyond all possibility of doubt that He is a real and the true power working through every cell of our being. That is all we need know, and that fact fills us up and makes us complete.

The Lord commanded us to be perfect, and it is only when we merge into the fabric of God's Being that we can be perfect—*Perfect, even as our Father in heaven is perfect.*

Nature is here to remind us of our insignificance; God is here to remind us of our greater nature, so that we can know our oneness with Him.

⸻

From the depths of your meditation, you may very well be inspired to do some great work; however, you must know God first for any endeavor to be truly successful. To know God, you transcend the desires, thoughts, and all preoccupations of the self. First, merge your little self in the great Self of God, then let all action flow from that high state. You will certainly be a blessing to this whole world as no other can be.

⸻

I give the love of God to all, and it is the most magnificent experience—a way of seeing God in action.

⸻

The more deeply you are immersed in God, the greater the good being done.

⸻

God is my guide, my friend, comforter, solver of problems, wise counselor, an ocean of love, and peace; my all in all. The most practical thing in my life.

⸻

Declare with all the power of God in you that you are determined to succeed. Feel the invisible forces in and around you as support, and when you meet obstacles, as you surely will with any worthwhile goal, feel those invisible forces aid and abet you as you overcome. When self-doubt assails you, as may happen to anyone doing something great, check inside for the rightness of your cause.

Do not seek to have God on your side, but rather know that you are on God's side through deepened meditation and intuition. Then proceed forward and be His instrument with true purpose in all things.

One great lesson is that when you make a determination and keep with it, especially when you invoke Divine Providence from the beginning, you attract invisible support for accomplishing your positive intention. Feel that you are not alone—God, the Masters, angels, and invisible forces respond to your clarity and uplifting purpose.

In this sense, there are no large or small goals, but only one goal, and that is the one in front of you now.

One of the "defaults" I now have is that in the face of difficulty, my mind immediately turns to God. "Oh Lord, You are the creator of this universe, You are of unlimited intelligence and unparalleled power. Change this situation, make it right, in accordance with the highest principles of wisdom, light, and love."

One sign of a spiritually charged environment is the ease with which one can feel God.

—◦◦◦—

When we turn to God, not just in despair, but for His will to operate directly in our lives, when we really open ourselves to Him, then we grow spiritually. Through that openness and making a connection with Him, we strengthen our union with Him in a most intimate and powerful way. Gradually, we come to see there is not a single second that we can draw a breath, have a thought, or have a sense of our being, without an active flow of His Divine Current.

—◦◦◦—

It is interesting how certain houses of God can have a dulling effect, some feel alright but not very powerful, then without fanfare, you are uplifted in the One true God; such was our experience as we were rooted in front of this lovely Synagogue. (The Mickve Israel Synagogue, established in 1878, is in Savannah, Georgia, USA.)

—◦◦◦—

God calls me inward; I allow full sway to His magnetic current . . . Truly, my life is not my own; He dictates what is to be done and not done. Whatever my, or others', expectations may be, His will reigns supreme. And, there is no place I would rather be.

Through these past many days, He has periodically continued to place me between the grinding forces of universal good and evil, and at the same time, He gives me such great bliss. Most often, even when He gives me some difficult task to do, He also gives me so greatly of Himself: inner assurance, blissful joy, and a keen understanding that this is all His will. Be it ever so!

❧

Wherever I have gone, God is present, within and without. Both in temples made by humans and Cathedrals of Nature, the sound of Aum/Amen and the Light of the Infinite have been in abundance. In all places, we have found God's helping hand through timely advice, direction, a caring comment, or friendly word. And, of course, His Divine Presence felt within has made the Infinite Beloved a constant feature throughout our pilgrimage.

❧

We seek out God Omnipresent beyond form, and on the way up, we are inspired by realized masters and saints, and rightfully so. Going beyond all form, we find God is all-pervasive, everywhere present.

In the universal vison, we find His voice being spoken through all: a child, someone in ignorance, and most lovingly from His perfected ones.

❧

The name Medicine Hat has a very interesting origin. The Blackfoot nation tells of an event that happened a long time ago. It was a bitter winter with starvation howling at the door. The Council of Elders gathered to discuss the matter. They decided a brave young man should be sent to a special place known as the "breathing hole," an opening in the ice of the Saskatchewan River where the Great Spirit was known to be present. After many days of arduous travel, the young man finally arrived there. He made camp and settled into fasting and prayer in order to summon the spirits. After his intense prayer, the Great Spirit appeared as a serpent. The serpent told the young man to spend the night on a small island (Strathcona). He was told, "In the morning when the sun lights the cut-banks, go to the base of the great cliffs and there you will find a bag containing medicines and a saamis (holy bonnet)." It was a hat to be worn only during battle. It would ensure victory. Aided by the saamis, the young man found food to save his starving people—he became a great Medicine Man.

This story has many interesting symbols, and I see in it a tale that contains tremendous inner meaning for the mystic. For the seeker of truth, the dark winter and starvation is the darkness of ignorance—not having joy and enlightenment which feeds the soul. The Council of Elders means inner direction, and the young warrior represents a newly-formed intention. The breathing hole is pranayama, a breathing exercise done in prayer and meditation. Pranayam kriya breaths and deepened meditation awaken the Great Spirit in the form of a serpent—the transformational kundalini force in the spine. The arising of the serpent force makes it possible to see the morning light—the great light seen in the ajna, or point between the eyebrows. The "bag of medicines" is the powerful spiritual uplifting energies coursing through the body and healing it of spiritual sickness or ignorance.

The bonnet of feathers or a hat is the consciousness lifted up to the top of the head, or what in yoga is called the sahaswara, the thousand-petalled lotus (such "hats" are used to symbolize uplifted consciousness, such as the tall hat of the pope, or the crown worn by a king). This medicine hat, given by the serpent, assures the warrior victory, assures that the spiritual aspirant will have the power to overcome the ignorance of separation from the Great Spirit in the "battle" of spiritual practice. All the people are then fed by the continuous flow of dynamic spiritual energy and consciousness flowing throughout the entire system—feeding all the people.

Thus, I find encoded in this ancient story a clear trail leading to spiritual illumination for a Medicine Man or a spiritual adept. Truth is universal, and it is fascinating and inspiring to know that it is, and has been, available to those who sincerely seek it in all parts of the world. Stories around the globe are adapted to the physical and social environment of the aspirant, but Truth is one.[5]

—❦—

Particular places bear greater vibrational weight; they radiate more life, and have a presence that is undeniable.

—❦—

One of the great things about saints and realized masters is that their divinized lives become allegories for realization: blueprints surcharged with divine consciousness for those who meditate deeply upon them. His or her life and experiences become a gateway to the Infinite—such is the grace of a great spiritual master.

---

5   Medicine Hat is a town in Alberta, Canada.

There is much written by saints and realized masters as to what the goal of spiritual practice is; however, no matter how perfect the words are for its description, there is no replacing actual God-contact and having direct experience of those realized states of consciousness.

You have been taught the truth by the greatest of spiritual masters; you are on the path to become a spiritual master yourself, and you have spiritual brother and sisters to help you on your way—these are the greatest blessings, and more than ample reason to have gratitude every moment of every day.

The story of God-incarnate unfolds. And it all begins in humble and wondrous beginnings on that holy night that promises so much. Be watchful for those portents that come to the surrendered and the humble. Listen for the celestial sounds of sacred watches; look for the blessed star that announces a new life in God; feel those powerful forces in motion in heaven and on earth; and be among the faithful looking to their Lord of Christly Divine Intelligence that guides them into union with the Holy Ghost (Divine Mother) and their Heavenly Father through the awakened Son of God within.

Everyday powers can easily be taken for granted, but I know without a doubt that God is the Source of every power that flows through this and every form. Having right relationship with power enables me to be in right relationship with my Creator. Power, like so many attributes of God, is then taken off the altar of false gods to be worshiped—bringing lasting peace and harmony to the Soul.

⸺⧟⸺

From the very beginning, through the middle parts, and all the way to its completion, God supplies all that you require to have the causal idea, the positive energy, and all you need for the accomplishment of your intention.

⸺⧟⸺

Open yourself to the unlimited resources of God and feel that abundance is flowing to you through creative ideas, the right help from others, new energy infusion, and material resources—all flowing to you, through you and out to the world from you. You are His instrument, and God delights in making you His co-creator.

⸺⧟⸺

It is the power of our thought and devotion that brings God and the masters to us, that gives us an experience with them. Deepened thought and devotion act as a magnet and makes them real.

The living Presence of these masters is the greatest of blessings to all whose minds are attuned to them.

We may have actual and direct experience with God or any of His saints and realized masters.

We may have actual and direct experience with God or any of His saints and realized masters.

Lahiri Mahasaya said, to think of Babaji with reverence releases a blessing to you: and so it is with all the great Ones.

To think of Master with total devotion will draw him near, will make you know that his grace and blessings are flowing to you; they will change you and draw you closer to God in body, mind, and soul.

Let us be inspired by Master and plug into the universal current that God is constantly sending out to this vast creation. Know that the only limit is our willingness and our growing capacity. Let us link our consciousness onto the powerful engine of Master through reading his words, thinking upon him, meditating upon the endless divinity that animated him in life; when you merge into him, you merge into the same Infinite Spirit he loved so much. God bless Master, and God bless the Work he came to do—to awaken all of us, all of creation to the Presence of our most perfect Creator.

The Master Jesus' life is one of perfect love for God, and the resurrection must be seen to its transcendental perfection. How rare and beautiful is that final journey. And how greatly the Master beckons to us, prods us, even pleads with us to follow—so that we may know what he knows, experience what he experiences, to be what he has become.

When we enter the spiritual way of seeing things, we seek to transfer our looking for assurance, safety, and order from this world to our growing union with God. But, as Mother affirms, Rome was not built in a day, and neither do individuals attain God-realization overnight. It is a process certainly, and one we seek to quicken. As Master said: Do not go by the bullock-cart method but take the airplane route. Through deepened God-experience, we recognize that the inner assurance of knowing God is the only constant in life—for everything that is born will die; everything that is created will one day disappear.

As Master said, "The same God that is in me, is also in you." We call upon that same God—the tremendous power, upliftment, and intelligence that made it possible for Master to do all he did—and that Divinity ignites in us the qualities of the all-powerful One.

We met two saints in Inda: The "touch" of these saints did not come through physical touch, nor was it their words, as these exchanges were not laced with much conversation; rather, it was the touch of their being—the touch of God in them that transmitted itself and continues to transmit its eternal message of purity, love, and joy that is God.

I bow at the feet of these luminaries. They are not famous or known because they attract large crowds, but they know God, and give what they know freely, without constraint or thought of what saint or organization you belong because they see God in you.

————

Yogis have specialized for millennia in observation and conscious use of life-force prana. Master Yogananda brought to the West a rational understanding of this force, based on his own experience. He also drew on traditions explained to him by his great guru Sri Yukteswarji, who was in turn taught by Lahiri Mahasaya, who was in turn taught by Babaji.

————

To merge into God means you merge into the Source of His eternal Being. In experiencing your union with God, you know Babaji, and Jesus, and the Soul of every exalted God-realized master. As Lahiri Mahasaya said: "Why do you want to come here to see this bag of bones? Focus your attention upon the Kutastha Chaitanya, the point between the eyebrows, and experience me directly."

CRLO

In hindsight, I can see that I was drawn by a guiding intelligence that gradually revealed my purpose. At first, it was an inarticulate knowing, and through sporadic experiences, which started to form into something more focused. My Guru drew me to herself, and she gave me the template for a blazing purpose, much of which was far beyond my grasp at the time—she was both a distant guiding star and she lit the ground in front of me to take learning-steps into a new world.

Let us take the lead from Papa, from Mother, and the great Ones who have gone before us to help make us know that union with the Beloved is our rightful inheritance.[6] He awaits us so that we might turn to Him so that He can embrace us, and make us His own. Be it so!

On both a human and a spiritual level, kinship in Spirit is of superior value.

As I sat cross legged on my meditation blanket, the master, Lahiri Baba Mahasaya, appeared before my inner vision, haloed in Light. He slowly descended from a levitation height and touched the carpet in front of me. I spontaneously bowed at his feet, and to my astonishment, I felt the flesh-and-blood touch of his feet. The master was

---

6   In each case, "Papa" refers to Swami Ramdas from Anandashram, Kerala, India.

not there in vision only, but in body. In my wonderment, I did not utter a word, but the master smiled a blessing and then the atoms of his body disbursed. Oh, what a wondrous feeling remained long after the master's body had left.

———∞———

He was born into, and lived, a human life, and Master, most notably, attained divine liberation. As such, his birth is truly worthy of celebration. Through his words, music, poetry, and his magnificent example, he continues to teach us about universal yoga—or union with God. Through his ongoing emanation of vibrations, he is actively lifting all attuned souls into higher consciousness so that struggling aspirants may become what they are—one with God.

———∞———

The purpose of spiritual masters being in this world—to be transmitting stations for the purifying and uplifting power of Divine Consciousness.

———∞———

God will spontaneously pour His power through this form—I feel it go out to individuals, families/groups, and out to the world as a whole. As I say, it is fascinating to observe what Divine Intelligence and Power does in and around this form.

———∞———

To feel that we have a friend in God makes our heart glow. God laughs with us, cries with us, enjoys a sunny day with us, and commiserates on rainy days. Our Divine Friend is the only one who can be with us always: from birth of the body to its last breath, before we come into this incarnation and far beyond when we continue our adventure. God creates us, so He knows us more intimately than perhaps we know ourselves—so there is nothing to hide.

Feel God's grace, even now, picking us up and helping us to put one foot in front of the other. That even when the bridge carrying the heavy weight moans and groans, His grace is supporting us in doing His will; His strength is ours; His grace is flowing in our veins and sinews, and His wisdom is directing us. All is in His loving hands.

We have no where we need go, no one we need to meet; we have only to go inside with full awareness and put our complete attention upon God and the masters, and we have all we need, and all that we will ever need, right inside of us.

Latent spiritual awareness can be awakened in you not because you have recently had such an experience, but because a great spiritual potential is sleeping in you and can be awakened by Masters. They awaken that sleeping giant of your God-self and puts you in touch with previously unknown realms. The awakened giant in Mother and Swamiji wakes up the sleeping giant in you![7]

———∞———

The spiritual master sows a seed in the aspirant, the power of God in the master warms the "oven" of consciousness for that one, making the conditions right; for the "the whole is leavened:" the three bodies, the physical, astral, and causal.

———∞———

This early morning, Saturn is bright, but Venus is truly blazing on the forehead of the eastern sky. The Big Dipper stands mighty, always pointing us to the North Star for direction, and Orion's belt and sword ever reminds me of Arjuna, the faithful warrior on the spiritual battlefield.

———∞———

In my soul, I walk with each one God has given me; I slog through the muck, I strain at the climb, and I glory in newfound vistas with each one of you. It is my greatest privilege to share in the toils but also to stand alongside you on glorious peaks of realization. It is the best of lives, the noblest of goals, and the most fulfilling of accomplishments to go to God together.

———∞———

---

7   Whenever denoted, "Swamiji" refers to Swami Satchidananda of Anandashram, Kerala, India.

Know that I hold you in my heart, and that in God there is no separation in time nor space—only oneness, only union in God.

———∞———

It is through His Omniscience that I feel you living your lives, taking sure and courageous steps towards God-realization.

———∞———

The hand of God is ever with us in the most loving way.

———∞———

There is a swell of spiritual consciousness that is lifting us higher.

———∞———

Individual will, attuned to Divine Will, makes for our greatest advancement.

———∞———

There is no greater realization that can be had; feel the wings of Spirit lift you to this abode of Bliss, in order to know what I am conveying to you.

———∞———

Sacred forces are at work in our life. The more we consciously access that fact, the greater God will reveal what we have come to express of His Light, Love, and Intelligence.

As aspirants, we too must take responsibility for making our best effort, to recognize the value and synergy of being on a team of devotees, ("For where two or three are gathered in my name, there I am in the midst of them" (Matthew 18:20), and the guru-coach helps us to make superlative individual and collective effort, ever directing us toward being victorious—that we might all become one with God and help lift this world into higher consciousness.

LEAVING THE PHYSICAL WORLD

When someone naturally leaves the physical world, when that is the case, you know there is no reason to grieve for that soul, for that one is now free of his or her physical frame, known to be like a heavy, lead, overcoat in comparison to the lightness of being in spirit. When in the body, one is normally limited to the five senses. Now in spirit, he or she is free and awareness is immeasurably greater; more closely attuned to divine emanations.

You may experience pure joy for that soul that soars beyond this physical world, even as you might for a bird that has been long caged and is now able to fly free.

———※———

When you remain mindfully conscious of Spirit through a loss, it purifies the mind. The death of someone close to you is a stern reminder that you are a "renter" in this body, not a "buyer;" one day death will come to claim you as well, and this clarity can lead to wisdom. When a death makes you go deeper to find comfort or answers, then you also grow spiritually. The choice of how you deal with death of the body is up to you; may you always choose the higher calling and be blessed.

———※———

When, not if, you have loss in your life, remember to be conscious in this process and let it draw you closer to

Divine Consciousness, fulfilling the great truth spoken by the great Galilean Master: blessed are they that mourn.

—❦—

Without knowing the eternal nature of the soul, and your ability to pass feelings through, grief may very well end up entrapping you. Your inability or unwillingness to let the feelings go will trap them in your mind and body, and you will endure unending torture of painful loss as they cycle through your mind and body, again and again. This hell is not required, nor is it wanted by the one who has passed.

—❦—

You will in all likelihood have some reaction to the death of a loved one, although it is not absolutely necessary. For instance, you may, through your connection with God, feel direct awareness of the individual soul as that one moves into his or her new life and there is no loss of connection either with the person or with God, and thus no sense of loss, no sorrow.

—❦—

We sometimes think that we exist only in one form; for instance, this physical body, to the exclusion of any other at any one time. The truth is, we simultaneously have all bodies available to us at all times; it is just that usually we are focused on the physical form and remain oblivious of the more subtle forms.

—❦—

The soul operates through the physical form of a human body, and when disease makes the body unresponsive, the consciousness of the soul remains unchanged, although it cannot continue to fully operate in the body as before.

＊＊＊

When an accomplished spiritual master senses that the time is right, he or she slip the bonds of the human body for the last time and enters into the realm of light and realization as a freed being—without necessity for returning to the earthly realm to fulfill unmet desires. For it is said that full spiritual realization answers all the heart's desires, leaving nothing for the master except to think, do, and say, as Divine Will directs. God chooses the moment for this final ascension, a well-known path by the master who "dies daily" in Christ Consciousness.

＊＊＊

While there will certainly be sorrow for those remaining behind, for the master, there is blissful release and the certain knowledge that he or she has fulfilled this earthly mission. Through our focus upon such an ascended masters, we attune ourselves to their divine consciousness and thus their grace may impart a blessing upon us.

＊＊＊

I suffer not just for my soul's sake, but for all creation. For the lifting of one link of life's chain, lifts all. "Oh Lord, when will this end?" And Grace answers, "When every contaminant has been scoured from the cup, so that nothing of

the three lower natures will sour My wine of pure Spirit."
Thus am I nailed. In this way I suffer. But it is the suffering
to end all suffering. The bridge may groan under a tremendous load coming over it, but still, it stands. And if
this body were to drop off when the work is done? What
of it! I have an eternal reward that surpasses the life of
this body in the way the sun's light is greater than the
firefly.

—◈◈◈—

When we drop-the-body, we then report to the supreme
Creator, who is no respecter of title, money, or position—all stand equally before the all-knowing One. Only
one thing will count: the quality of our inner self—built
with a lifetime of what we think, say, and do—our consciousness that exudes from our innermost being. That is
what lasts, and that is what counts.

—◈◈◈—

In God-consciousness, all people, past and present, feel
near and dear.
    When you use the feeling of loss to deepen connection
with your infinite Beloved, then wounds are healed and
loss becomes gain.

—◈◈◈—

Stillness is one of the great virtues of spiritual consciousness. Some might associate stillness with death; a dead
body does not breathe, move, or show signs of life. A
yogi, one in union with God, may not breathe, or very

shallowly, may not show signs of life, yet such stillness is the opposite of death—dead, perhaps to the world for a while, but by no means the inertness of a dead body.

—⊸∞⊶—

Master was not "taken away," rather, he is now permeating every particle of space, in every flower's fragrance and the golden sunset. Even closer, he is in your heart and can be heard in your soul's whispers. Master is ever with the attuned soul, ever waiting for you to follow him into your eternal oneness with your Heavenly Father and Divine Mother.

—⊸∞⊶—

Yogacharya David at the Snake and Columbia
River Prayag, Washington State, USA., 2017.

Joy

GRATITUDE

No matter where we go or how far we go, all we have to do, is to think of Anandashram, and the peace, joy, and love of God and His devotees will forever ring in our hearts with deepest gratitude. Om Sri Ram Jai Ram Jai Jai Ram! Victory to God, Victory to the Light, and may Universal love and service forever reign in the world as its motto and practice.

When your heart softens in gratitude, you feel close to God; in feeling close to God, you feel peace, inner assurance, and bliss! This is the finest gift you can give to yourself and to others; it will truly make the day special.

A natural result of a conscious connection with God is gratitude. It is reciprocal as well; a feeling of gratitude brings God closer. To make a day of thanksgiving truly meaningful, take time to remember the many blessings for which you are grateful.

Even if life is rough for you right now, list those things in life for which you are truly grateful and deliver them at the feet of God; feel the connection with the Infinite grow in sacred, heartfelt joy.

As I wrap the shawl around me in the early morning hours, I am filled with quiet excitement at the prospect and privilege of delving into Nirguna (expressionless) Spirit. In this moment, I am totally free to be with God: I close my eyes, still my breath, and experience the ever-perfect Spirit. Oh, what privilege is mine! But not a privilege as a miser might have, for I know that all willing souls might join me in this groundswell of spiritual thrill that captures my soul, brings tears to my eyes, and puts me in touch with the all-pervasive Reality.

"Oh Lord, with constant gratitude, my heart heaves in the ebb and flow of the ocean of Thy love."

───∞───

Gratitude overflows the heart. Oh, what gracious spiritual breezes waft through body, mind, and soul. The wealth of a yogi is in this Presence, this indescribable peace and joy. The world exists, certainly it does. With its ups and downs, pleasures and pains, yet all pales in comparison to this exquisite bliss.

The larger God looms into the foreground, the more insignificant becomes the variegated nature of the world. Now the joys of the world are pleasing reminders of God's little gifts, and the pains are promptings to look to the Infinite for comfort and strength. All of these plays of opposites are but a small subset of the grand overarching Spirit. Ah, such awareness does bring gratitude into the life of the devotee; life, love, finding spontaneous joy in the soul are reasons enough.

───∞───

As a spiritual aspirant, I also look back to the source of grace that has blessed my life. I offer flowers of my devotion with all love and gratitude as I bow to the feet of my Guru-lineage, as well as realized saints and sages around the world. These valiant souls left known lands to explore vast new realms of spiritual consciousness. These intrepid pioneers gave everything of what they were for this quest, and then went on to produce spiritual progeny to help guide future generations of realized souls.

—⚬⚬⚬—

The Ten Commandments tell us to honor both father and mother, for it is in gratitude to these souls that we acknowledge that we have the opportunity for this present incarnation. Our parents made possible our very survival when young. They gave us much of the strength we have, and so many mannerisms and habits are linked to these headwaters from which we have sprung.

Even if we are not standing in front of a headstone, we can silently offer flowers of prayerful thankfulness for the good we have received. And then looking forward, be determined to add even greater strength and awareness for ourselves and for future generations.

—⚬⚬⚬—

I want to wish all mothers a special blessing of love and gratitude. Without mothers this human race would vanish! By going into the jaws of death to bring forth new life, a mother only begins her journey of motherhood. And there is an even greater role for all mothers, for all women—each one is a manifestation of the Divine Mother.

To all women, I bow at your feet in love and gratitude for your unique contributions as expressions of the beloved Divine Mother.

———

Either you can focus on what is wrong to the exclusion of the blessings you have, or you can cultivate gratitude and count your blessings.

———

Do not let moods, concerns, fears, or unbridled desire make you deaf and blind to everyday joy.

Find micro-moments of joy all through the day, string these moments together and make a beautiful pearl necklace of God-joy.

———

God is joy, and unless we are actively participating in joy, then we are starving our soul of the very nourishment it absolutely needs.

———

I am called to meditate; the messenger is a thrill up the spine, a rarified tingling sensation all around the cranium. I sit and joy bubbles up from deep within; a smile creases itself across my face and love pours out through the eyes. The eyes close—life is lifted up the spine to the point between the eyebrows. Then, it slides through the ajna like it's moving through a super soft silken fabric. A tiny fragment of awareness feels Divine Light unfolding in the brain like so many petals of a rounded lotus. That too recedes and awareness is beyond the body, merging into all-space. No thought encroaches into that realm sublime. Pure awareness, slipping the bonds of heaven and earth where only resplendent Self exists.

Oh Master, Oh Mother, saints of all religions, this is what you have come to awaken in us. All else is simply stuff of the mind. Oh Lord, You are the moving and motionless Spirit, the author of all that is and so much more. I melt in gratitude. Om Gurus, Om Sri Ram.

───※───

Experiencing divine Grace begets a natural state of gratitude, even as a sense of gratitude brings about a feeling of closeness with our Creator.

───※───

Giving gratitude brings about balance in your perspective; looking at all the ways you have grown, advanced, and become more empowered! Taking legitimate pride for what you have done circles you, the sincere aspirant, right back to the source of your accomplishments—your life in God.

───※───

God has given us each other to make spiritual progress with and to give mutual support—what a tremendous gift that has been in my life. For that, and for all the unbounded grace God gives, I am deeply grateful.

The gift of spiritual awakening is the ultimate gift for which we are grateful. Just getting started on this path to Self-realization is of great import; how many darkened lifetimes have we spent in ignorance and suffering with no spiritual understanding?

Oh Lord, You are the all in all. You have taken your pilgrims upon this journey so that we might know that Your Spirit is to be found in all places, and all people. This vast creation is Your playground, and while it can be rough play; nevertheless, You are ever-present—a Guide, Comforter, and Protector for Your devotees. Certainly, life can take a deleterious turn from a human standpoint, but when seen correctly, it is only You, only You.

Oh Beloved, take the scales from our eyes, unstop our ears, and open our hearts so that we may see only You, hear only You, love only You.

Spiritual practice keeps the devotee from falling into ordinary, humdrum existence.

Bring to mind the micro-reasons for gratitude in your daily life: when you have enough money for food and shelter, it is no small thing; have the power to walk, talk, and carry on in your life, is a miraculous blessing; daily, you have an enormous opportunity to fill your life with gratitude.

———&———

Cultivate your gratitude conversation with God until it is the most natural thing in the world, and you will find that life is, perhaps, made up of a very few big events that many people look for to validate something to be grateful for, but, easily, has unending micro-events in everyday existence that the gratitude habit makes you aware of, and brings to you joy and true happiness for yourself and those around you.

———&———

Everything works for ultimate good, and through intense focus on God, the soul is lifted out of duality and is established in bliss. For spiritually aspiring sadhakas, this is the ultimate for which to feel gratitude: to know that you have the Goal of goals in mind (a remarkable purpose), and the capacity to achieve this Goal in this lifetime is cause for great celebration and joy—a true day of thanksgiving.

———&———

Notice micro-events all through the day, then say, "Lord, what a wonderful thing to be able to do: to look at the sky, breathe the air, give someone a smile, strive for a goal; this life is a miracle in action, a joy to behold! Even the things that dissatisfy me, You have put it into my mind so that life can be better, so that I can work for improvement; for that inspiration to improve, I give thanks."

———&———

Gratitude and God are definitely closely linked.

—⊗⊗⊗—

Start a conversation with God that lasts throughout your waking hours. Look for micro-events that you might normally take for granted, and then express your gratitude to your Creator for it.

—⊗⊗⊗—

When feeling close to God gratitude comes naturally; it lifts our mood and makes us feel closer to God—gratitude and God are definitely closely linked.

—⊗⊗⊗—

When you have challenges of health, prosperity, and in relationships, inwardly commune with your infinite Beloved giving thanks, knowing He knows all that you need, and His great love and desire for your good to come to you is even now doing so.

Giving thanks is an affirmation for what is even now coming to you in multifarious ways.

—⊗⊗⊗—

Thank you, Guru-lineage, and true saints and spiritual masters, for showing us the Way—for being the examples of right action. It is not the easy path of no rules, but it is the path that leads to freedom. My eternal gratitude to blessed Guru and Guru-lineage for being the Way for all of us.

—⊗⊗⊗—

Jesus, the great master, came with a unifying message for all humankind: we are all children of the one Father-God, and through the perfection of our love for our Father, and for all His children everywhere, we might rise up in oneness with Him. Let us meditate upon his life and message, and thus be transformed into his perfect likeness.

Simplicity, perfect joy, keen insightful wisdom, and purity of thought, word, and action are all defining virtues of this great master. I thank God and Babaji for the day Lahiri Baba was born into a human body, for the great gift that he is, for the Kriya Yoga he taught, and the supreme wisdom he freely gave to all sincere aspirants who sought shelter at his holy feet. May we too find such shelter and be led into the highest states of realization by this supreme master, our para-param guru, Lahiri Mahasaya.

I bow in gratitude to my ancestors, to all our ancestors, and affirm that with our hard work, we may pass better lives down to future generations, and that the day will come when wars and terrorism are but memories, and the only "trumpet calls" we hear are the ones that awaken our souls to God.

Today, I give honor to my father and grandfathers, and our beloved Father in Heaven. To my father and grandfathers, I feel such gratitude for all your hard work that conveyed your love for family far more eloquently than you ever expressed in words. And, for my Father in Heaven, may we all feel the same intimacy that Jesus felt in relationship with You—such love, care, and closeness. And for all of you fathers today, who work and strive to make your families safe, secure, and loved, I give you thanks.

———

Let us love the life God has given us, and while we can make plans to build a future that serves us perfectly, we also love life in the process—what we have right here, in this place, and at this time.

The love and gratitude for what we have now opens the door for God to create, through us, all that He wishes to express in our life. And His will for us, even when it challenges us to our core, is, in truth, pure ananda-joy.

———

It is one thing to give thanks for what has been given, but to give thanks for that which is to come opens the floodgates for grace to flow to you.

———

May every moment of every day be filled with gratitude for the greatest gift of all—the living Presence of our Infinite Beloved.

———

Thank you, Lord, for giving me the awareness of Your Presence, for in that deep connection with You, I have everything that You are. I live in the prime simplicity of Your Being—I am merged in You, and You in me. And through Your all-powerful Presence, You may fulfill Your will for me, and for this world.

When you choose joy, you choose God, and when you choose God, you choose joy.

For one who suffers the effects of past actions in body, mind, or soul, we feel compassionate understanding for that one—we feel the fullness of God's love flowing through our own heart in omniscient empathy.

A feeling of love and devotion for God gives us a sense of connectedness and removes the feeling of isolation that can come with circumstances in which we had a lack of control.

Be conscious for that which makes us grateful to our Creator, we can be aware of more than the challenges we face, and we can see unnumbered things to be grateful for.

The value of these yoga methods cannot be overstated. Let us be filled with gratitude for God and Gurus and His Saints through whom His Grace flows.

———— ⟨⟩ ————

God's Will reigns supreme.

———— ⟨⟩ ————

MOTHER

t is through the Divine Mother that all creation has come into being; without Her there would be no expression of God. Therefore, we give great homage to the Divine Mother.

―∞―

Here on earth, Divine Mother is a much-desired form that may manifest in any number of expressions in India, Quan Yin (Guanyin) in China, or numerous variations the world over, as Her expressiveness knows no limit.

―∞―

In your spiritual journey, feel that God is looking after you as a solicitous mother would look after her child. Divine Mother is ever anxious that you be safe and comforted, that you know you have Her eternal love. Whatever you fill your mind with, you draw unto yourself.

Feel the tenderness and love of Divine Mother; have full awareness She is ever looking after you. Look into those soft, melting eyes and know She has ever loved you. Let Her solace ever make you know that you are Her child— that you are in Her, even as She is in you.

―∞―

Oh, my dear Swamiji, You have been so instrumental in what I have in God. I have often referred to You as my second Mother, Mother Hamilton being my first Mother.

With unbounded love and perseverance, you helped to chip away the dross that covered the Divine Light within this 'temple not made with hands.' My love and gratitude are endless, and I surrender myself to your holy feet. Om Sri Ram Jai Ram Jai Jai Ram.

⊷∞⊷

The Divine Ego is enabled to manifest all the attributes of God; for then, in truth, it may be said, "I and Thou are one." This great event is a tremendous boon to the world, for it brings all the purity of God into this physical realm in ways that are unique. Mother was, and is, just such a blessing for this world.

⊷∞⊷

I saw Mother with inner sight: she was beaming and more beautiful than I had ever seen her before. A radiant light went out from her in every direction as far as I could see. Through thought transference, she said, "Do you not know, I am now in my Light-body." And, indeed, she was, and is, a brilliant shining Light.

⊷∞⊷

In deepest reverence, I bow at the feet of my beloved Guru. My prayer for you: that you might also receive glints of Mother's pure God-light, and thereby be lifted higher and higher, until you, like her, merge into our Infinite Beloved and ever know that you and your Heavenly Father-Divine Mother are ever one.

A mother will draw the soul that is destined for her through her magnetism of karma, and a spiritual teacher will draw students through his or her pure spiritual magnetism. It was for the purpose of meeting Mother that I came into this incarnation, and like a powerful magnet, Mother drew me to herself.

Blessings for the human sacrifices made by all mothers, and may you know the absolute purity of the Divine Mother within you. Om, Amen.

When we really think about it, new life is absolutely a miracle, and no new human life is possible without a mother.

It is the Divine Mother who has manifested as this entire universe—a loving, compassionate, exacting Mother who seeks to awaken us to the fact that it is She behind the mask of humanity—nay, behind all creation, if we only have the wit to lift the veil and know Her in truth and reality.

VICTORY TO THE LIGHT

Make your life an epic in which Light triumphs over darkness, discover vast realms of Spirit within, and you are a blessing to all whom you meet—now, that is a story worth telling, and a life worth living!

———

Bhakti, loving devotion, is said to be the easiest path to God because there is nothing more powerful than loving remembrance. In that divine state of mind, it is not work to think of your Beloved; it is no trouble to do something in service to the One; rather, it gives you great joy! You are enthusiastic to discover what your Beloved likes. You are charmed by everything the Infinite says and does; it is the greatest love affair you will ever know.

———

Om Sri Ram Jai Ram Jai Jai Ram: Victory to God, Victory to the Light for this entire world. Your pure Light is radiating through so many souls here. What a rare thing to have such continuous illumined masters in this lineage, Papa, Mataji, and You, my dear Swamiji. May Anandashram ever be a beacon of purity and Light for one and all. Om Sri Ram Jai Ram Jai Jai Ram!

———

Deep and sincere practice of meditation and God-remembrance is the antidote to worldly influence. When you feel drawn to the peace and bliss of God you find the world loses its allure. Just as when the body is cleared of an addictive substance, then even the thought of having that substance no longer has a hold on the individual, even so the devotee feeling the active joy of God does not yearn for the pleasures of the world.

Through pure vision, the Kingdom of Heaven is spread all over this earth, and with eyes to see, and ears to hear, it is unallayed joy to behold it. May you also know that kingdom as it manifests in your life, and may you feel His bliss, now and always.

Flame Exercise: When a thought comes to you and does not spark joy, then discard it. See with your mind's eye a flame 12 to 14 inches in front of you, then send the unwanted thought into this flame—the Light of God. See those thoughts you are discarding flowing into the flame. See the flame consume the thought and take it up and away—purified in those flames. In this way you can choose only thoughts that give you joy. Let everything else go. Moods, unhealthy desires, compulsions, and negativity can be gotten rid of, beginning now!

Decide to think only of Light, universal Love, and ever-new Joy, and change your life—never to be the same.

Make your life an epic in which Light triumphs over darkness, discover vast realms of Spirit within, and you are
a blessing to all whom you meet—now, that is a story
worth telling, and a life worth living!

My awareness moved out over a vast expanse, like light
catapulting from a sun out into vast space. Only this
"photon of light" expands and merges into the space into
which it is moving, and this "photon" knows unparalleled
joy in so doing.

What I can tell you is that God is fully present and
accounted for. His bliss is even now flowing through my
spine and brain and through all the cells of my body. Truly
there is nothing but He, even when there is weakness,
pain, or discomfort, it is all He!

When your life comes into balance and you have congru-
ity between Spirit, thought, word, and action, then you
have a credible claim on peace today.

I see the great adventure of this life as refining and purifying consciousness, to make it ready for a true New Birth.

I am to remain connected to the all-important inner-net; the power and intelligence of Divine Consciousness. With this connection streams His peace, joy, and direction. There is nothing more that I want or need. So, for what God has given me to do, for what He has given you to do, Victory to God!

Victory to the Light! For all sentient beings, everywhere!

—⊗⊗⊗—

No matter your situation, you have available to you micro-moments of joy. Do not let moods, concerns, fears, or unbridled desires make you deaf and blind to everyday joy. Your meditation is designed to bring out that joy. God remembrance is joy itself, and such joy is not dependent upon wealth, health, or situation—for God is transcendent to all such considerations.

—⊗⊗⊗—

Association with the Light will also make us into its own nature—unalloyed peace, joy, and unending freedom—if we only choose it.

—⊗⊗⊗—

Sri Yukteswarji said that we are emerging from dark ages into greater light. Mother added that the age of darkness we are coming out of was an unusually dark cycle from which it has been very difficult to emerge. The challenges are great, but the possibilities are even greater. Great souls can help lift this world into a new age of world peace and enlightenment.

———⊶⊷———

Om Sri Ram Jai Ram Jai Jai Ram: Victory to God, Victory to the Light for this entire world. Your pure Light is radiating through so many souls here. What a rare thing to have such continuous illumined masters in this lineage, Papa, Mataji, and You, my dear Swamiji. May Anandashram ever be a beacon of purity and Light for one and all. Om Sri Ram Jai Ram Jai Jai Ram!

———⊶⊷———

Come, rise up into the consciousness of Krishna, Christ, Yogananda, Mother; know the same state of awareness they know; be infused with the same power to bring light and healing to one and to all; immerse yourself into the bliss they too enjoyed. It is the reason they taught at all, so that you might be as they are in God. Come, receive your innate divinity and be one with your heavenly Father and Divine Mother.

———⊶⊷———

May Master Yogananda's light shine ever brighter, leading all sincere aspirants to the harbor of God-experience—eternal, ever-new Joy! Jai Guru.

———⊶⊷———

Spiritual masters attain a high state of consciousness in which they transcend the limitations of the five senses and the reasoning mind: they find themselves in states of bliss; have visions of light beyond that which the sun, or flame, brings to the eye; hear sounds that come from the depths of creation; and have a deep sense of knowing who and what they truly are that transcends the short human life-cycle here on earth. Much can be written to try and capture this high state, but none can be the final word on it.

From a human standpoint, the workings of nature can make one feel small. From a Divine perspective, it makes God extremely great. The human is definitely part of all that is; however, all that is is a marvel and more than the mind can contain.

To be in awe—to be in continual awe and wonder is to be close to God.

——— ❧ ———

The greatest gift we can give our beautiful lineage, along with the inspiration and grace we have received from so many saints the world over, is to strive with all of our hearts, strength, minds, and souls for attaining that most blessed state of consciousness wherein we know we are no longer separate individuals living in darkness, but that we have boldly stepped into the light, and we find the same light radiating in us that is so clearly seen in our guru-lineage. This is the greatest way to honor Guru Purnima Day. (Guru Purnima Day is observed on the day of the full moon in July to honor the importance of teachers.)

——— ❧ ———

Association with realized souls and those aspirants with burning zeal adds to the flame of enthusiasm and makes us burn bright. Reading or hearing inspired wisdom adds dry, seasoned wood. Making God-contact in deepened meditation, and singing His name throughout the day inflames the soul and makes it mad for God.

Love for God radiates Divine Light in us and helps others to burn brightly. The ego-mind of separation is consumed in this flame and the Divine Goal of Satchidananda—the eternal Self, full-consciousness, and bliss are now enjoyed, fulfilling our deepest heart's desire. The experiment is proved—we now know from our own experience that realizing God alone is the source of true and lasting happiness!

—————

Is our circle of love growing? Is our heart softer and more open? What is the trend of our mind—do we know God, and experience Him more and more? What is the use of saying we follow a spiritual path if our thoughts and actions do not increasingly manifest the truth we have been taught?

—————

We are to be good stewards of what we do know.

We know that when we act according to the highest light in any particular situation, He may find us fit instruments to do ultimate good. We know this because we feel Him working through us, thinking through us, acting through us, in perfect purity, and without a trace of self.

In this hand-in-glove relationship, we are at peace, we experience bliss, we know beyond all possibility of doubt that He is the real and true power working through every cell of our being—that is all we need to know.

God-realization is not the attainment of miraculous powers—it is ever-new joy. We all love to have God come
in super-ordinary ways, but really, miracles are small
potatoes compared to exploring His vast Being. The real
touchstone of God-experience is blissful joy.

Blessings, blessings for the unwritten pages that will be
filled with the unfolding days of each new year. May you
be a perfect conduit for the supreme Light of this world
to manifest through your every thought, word, and action.

There is nothing I love more than to see the unfolding
of the lotus-life of a God-expanding soul. I know that it
is not an easy journey: there are lofty peaks and dark
chasms, there are fair winds at your back, and slamming
storms that shudder you stem to stern, and there is the
guiding Eastern Star, and the Sirens who seductively call
you to destruction.

It is the greatest hero's journey ever told, and therefore, dangerous and uncertain, but also impregnated with
Grace-filled synchronicities, the tender mercies of Divine
Mother, and lightning flashes of wisdom from heavenly
Father. There is truly nothing more thrilling to me than
to be a participant/witness in this greatest of odysseys
with you.

My birthday (February 26): I blow out a candle of one, standing for the One eternal Being. With this expended breath, I project my prayerful wish for you: that you melt in His Spirit, swim in His ocean of Bliss, for His mind to mingle in your own, and for you to see and serve Him in all creation.

Oh Lord, it is You, Yourself, who has thought this birthday wish into my mind; therefore, it is Your wish and You must fulfill it for all your sincere lovers. For there is nothing, nothing greater in all the three worlds than to stand in Your Presence—This I wish and pray with all my heart for all of my and Your dear ones—and all be near and dear to You!

———❧———

God loves to express Himself, and thus gives rise to the idea of seeming separateness, but only so that pure Spirit may enjoy the play, the lila—and for no other reason. But enough talk! I am dissolving once again into that chamber of the infinite and eternal—let us plunge together into the sea of Pure Being, Consciousness, and Bliss—it is what an aspirant must do, so why wait another moment!

———❧———

Yes—declare freedom! Let us soar on wings like eagles and experience the soul's joy born of deepened meditation and love of God.

———❧———

When a creation becomes so attuned to higher thought and vibrational living, then a material world may simply transmute into pure spiritual Being—such things are possible and do happen. However, we are far from such harmony today—though we cannot discount that, like a rising flood, God's power can sweep over this earth and make it new. How my heart yearns for such upliftment for one and of all.

———

Recently, a devotee went through a serious operation. She said that while in recovery, she felt that she was in the hospital for some greater reason—she had deep conversations there with a young man with addiction problems, visited many on the ward, and was a bright light, and in fact the nurses gravitated to her room due to her calm and positive manner. When I was in the hospital, I too felt that this was my opportunity to pray for all those there, including the care givers. With the mind so busily engaged in bringing the Light of God to a situation, there was no time for worry!

———

There are many reasons why individuals become discouraged about life, some personal, some global. A negative-tamasic mood robs one of joy and draws a curtain between the soul and the true Self. We must have perspective in life.

Knowing that the Light perpetually shines in the darkness is the greatest reason for optimism, at all times and in all places.

———❧———

It is the one thing about God—He is not a thing of the past, or a story that becomes staid, but a deep well of living waters that brings new birth and new openings to the most tremendous gift ever given to all God's children.

———❧———

Through the news, we can come to believe this world is completely lacking in goodness and selflessness. My own experience is quite the opposite. I know that the vast majority of people are fundamentally good, and that there are shining soul-stars that light the darkness for us all. I think of all these luminous lights in the firmament of Spirit, and it makes me smile—most definitely it gives me a warm glow.

———❧———

As part of nature's outdoor cathedrals, it is one thing to admire its many beauties, but what stands out to me, are a couple of peaks that soar above us and shed their great presence each morning and throughout the day. It has been my experience that mountains, trees, rivers, lakes, and the land itself, emanate life-energy consciousness—there is no such place that is lifeless.

———❧———

Know that being made in the likeness and image of God, you too are a joyful creator. Make this year the greatest yet for being His instrument in manifesting His Light, His joy, and His positive creations—all done for the highest good of all.

I am wrapped in His ecstasy, and there is nowhere I would rather be. He wants me to be His witness, a reporter from the front lines of God-consciousness—to speak only the truth of what He gives me—what He reveals to me and makes me experience.

The yearning pain in the heart sets up a magnetism to which God must respond. Instead of trying to empty the mind of self only, which can have negative consequences, the positive thought of God fills the mind with light, love, and devotion—making for a healthy psychological outlook.

Victory to God—Victory to the Light—may unbounded love, and keen discrimination, ever guide the way for devotees, so that all may find the flawless way to the one infinite Lord.

Light is greater than darkness, love eradicates fear, and peace transcends mischief-making and turbulence.

Celebrating resurrection this time of year, the spring equinox, is wonderfully symbolic of the arisen consciousness. Locally, the daffodils are bursting into bloom. Like so many rays of golden suns, life is returning after slumbering in winter, seeds burst their bonds, and branches reach out for the light—new life, new hope, a renewed world.

As we meditate upon this miracle of nature, let us know that an even greater miracle is promised within—the resurrection of Divine Consciousness, that we may know our Heavenly Father in truth and reality.

—⊕⊕⊕—

Blessings for the Householder Yogi: Bless you and your home; make it a sanctuary that is a witness and a support to your aspiring spirit. As the petals of God-experiences unfold in your receptive soul, may they reveal the flower of Self-realization that lights your whole Being, your entire home, and fills all the world with His eternal splendor. Ever in God, Christ, Gurus.

—⊕⊕⊕—

What we must know; "wake up calls" come with a purpose—to wake us up!

The Vedas say: "Arise, Awake!" When all we have is taken away from us, then we must turn to God as our refuge, solace, comforter, and guide.

—⊕⊕⊕—

The inner stillness of the yogi comes with deepened meditation; the body becomes quiet and the mind enters into the great stillness—awareness continues, but the constant monologue of the mind stops. When I have been out cross-country skiing or snow shoeing, the swish or crunch of snow is all that makes noise. Suddenly, coming to a stop, the snowflakes quietly fall and there is total quiet, a hush is all around—a remarkable feeling. There is an element of that hush that is in this inner stillness, a feeling of magic almost, of awe that moves the soul.

Ultimately, every individual is led to the Light of his or her own soul.

God's bliss lives in every particle of space, and it lives in us.

The hero's journey is the sure way through darkened places and into the light. We are here to individually and collectively walk upon the path of the hero, to make our way to the portal of the Infinite, then to enter into that portal, and go beyond all that we have known before.

In truth, our life is the greatest story ever told; so, make it a good one; make it count.

Let us Bless ourselves by taking the spiritual adventure of a lifetime; let us be in the Know and get the Insider information that boosts our God-stock—it only ever goes up, and it never loses its value!

Oh, what a friend we have in God! So loyal, patient, with solace in heart and mind, when we come to Him in earnestness. To cultivate this friendship makes the Infinite available to us day and night: a witness to our trials, a collaborator in our tests, and a dispenser of joy when we accomplish something worthy.

Amazing may very well be one of those overused words that gets thrown into too many conversations—or, on the other hand, everything in this creation is truly amazing because it is all made up of God-stuff, and therefore is extraordinary from its very inception to its eventual end.

Let us practice, practice, practice until we are living in the "Spiritual Zone" and feel God's joyful presence within, until we are centered in our deeper Self, no matter our outer circumstances, and until our inborn dharma spontaneously guides us to the right action.

May the sacred time of celebrating the birth of Christ Consciousness into the world, and into the human frame, strengthen your resolve to be in seamless union with the ever-perfect Light of your Heavenly Father and Divine Mother.

Certainly, this world is here for us to enjoy, and part of that enjoyment is the variety of variegated expression. To bring all of these multifaceted creations under one roof requires a universal principle, and that is the presence of God, weaving a musical theme of bliss throughout all creation.

Let us find the bliss within that makes this promise a reality—even now, even now.

—◦◦◦—

May peace ring out from the inner depths of our humble soul, and may the promise of a divine child be born in us, bringing to life all of its fulfillment—for us and for all of humankind.

—◦◦◦—

I feel the wonder and the beauty of Thy glorious Presence in every part of my being. My heart is bursting with my love for Thee. My mind and my intelligence are radiant with Thy healing Light. I and my Father are One, blessed Spirit, I am He!

—◦◦◦—

Each new year brings the promise of the Second Birth to each one who sincerely applies himself or herself to living according to the highest Light he or she knows.

—◦◦◦—

Some people fear that if they go with God, they give up on having fun in life; their lives will be dull, staid, and constricted. How wrong they are! God, the intelligence that creates this universe, is the power behind all activities, and the pure essence of joy! This choice brings the most exciting and most challenging life.

God is ever-new joy and, therefore, is always the right choice.

—⊷⊷—

Bliss changes your life in all ways good; joy fills you from the inside out. So, make your environment, your family, your friends, and your life align with God's joy, and He will guide you perfectly in all your ways. Blessings.

—⊷⊷—

May He lift us into the awareness that His all-loving, all-knowing Presence is with us no matter what 'space' we may be in, or what mask He may wear.

—⊷⊷—

This play of God is a fun reminder that no matter the appearances of a thing, God is at work. Sometimes, we are in on the plan, sometimes it is simply knowing there is a plan and that it is all being worked out according to Divine Will. All is in His Keeping. All is in His will.

—⊷⊷—

See every person, every situation in life filled with God's light and life, working its way towards His perfection. Your light can extend out all over this whole world, and even beyond. That is a mighty purpose!

—∞—

And this is my Saint Valentine's wish for you my dear One, that you may drink to your heart's content from Living Waters of Spirit; that your heart may run full to overflowing with love for God and all creation. That when you do an act of charity, it is first an act of love, an action that is a natural outcome of omnipresence. And when you are the receiver of someone's loving act, that you receive the love behind the act and are conscious of it first. In this way, it is truly God giving to God.

It is in that spirit that you please me most in receiving all the love of God that is, even now, overflowing my heart and that I see flowing out to you now. "Your Valentine."

—∞—

A smile grows through inner radiance, love glows in my heart, and peace is felt within and without; these are signs of being on the right track.

—∞—

Sri Yukteswarji, an incarnation of wisdom, is a flawless compass guiding us to the Eternal. Such wisdom can be very strict, crushing our meandering dreams and ruthlessly severing our attachments. This is all done without malice but with the greatest love and solicitude. In fact, all that this great God-man did was done to bring about a revelation that all creation is an explosion of Ananda-Bliss—and as such, the realization that we are part and parcel made up of sacred Joy.

You have both the wisdom of the wise in you, and you are a being of bliss without end. This is what Sri Yukteswarji came to awaken in Master, and in us all.

—⚬⚬⚬—

One simply cannot measure a spiritual master by outward signs, although those signs may give a hint of his or her inner glory. We love to hear stories of any great saint, but to hear the story alone is a bit like looking into a room from the other side of a glass window—nice, but not the same as being in the room itself.

—⚬⚬⚬—

Peace is not something that occurs at any particular time; peace is an ever-existent state of being that can be made self-evident at any time and at all times.

—⚬⚬⚬—

May the tender and all-powerful Divine Incarnation of Christ be born in you.

—⚬⚬⚬—

It is good to remember that God-realized souls live human lives; they endure what everyone goes through at one time or another. They do this to show us that our humanness is not a bar to experiencing God. Rather, we may feel that it is God living His life through us, and therefore, everything—pleasure and pain, happiness and sadness—comes from the one Source of all that is.

God plays through us like a fine instrument, hitting any range of notes of His own choosing—for all is made from the musical streams of Ananda/Bliss.

———❧———

Let us cheerfully meet the world and know God as your sole (Soul) support, comforter, and guide.

———❧———

Just a touch of this bliss I am feeling could change indifference into unending awe.

———❧———

Live, breathe, and act according to active Divine Will. Victory is now ours through our surrender; the falsity of ego is but a past dream and we love life because all of life is now seen as a process of evolution in becoming Divine. Life itself is exciting because we are filled with bliss and wonder at all the works God does within and without.

———❧———

My heart cries out to awaken all to this Mystery of Happiness that heals the world of its woes.

———❧———

God is equally present everywhere; it is just that he seems more equally Present in some places than others!

———

Peace is not something that occurs at any particular time; peace is an ever-existent state of being that can be made self-evident at any time and at all times.

———

Offending individuals may be in our thoughts and prayers, seeing them as the children of God as they truly are in their immortal souls. One day, they will grow into who and what they are in God, but for today, they may be kept at an arm's distance—all the while, in heart, mind, and soul, they are held in the pure light of being just as God created them from the foundations of this universe.

———

We have all come from "tough stock", and the many losses and difficulties of those previous generations can be passed down through families—it can explain much in what may seem unexplainable symptoms. Then, you add on the layers of past lifetimes a soul has experienced during this dark Kali Yuga; for example, the emotional charges of past life experiences lurking deep in the sub-conscious mind—all building. This complex weave of the psyche reveals why unexpected challenges can seem to occur from thin air, as well as unexplainable strengths and talents we simply come with, fully intact, from birth.

———

Your life is an expression of infinite nature; you are meant to live in freedom, joy, love, and light. To tune into this greater Source, you must rise above your determined beliefs that you are small and your problems are big. It is true that on a human level, many things can come at you, and challenges can really stretch you, but you are not a human-self only.

You must remember that you are a child of the Infinite, and in remembering this, you claim access to the realms of your greater Self.

———∞———

How greatly the Master loves all humanity.

There are none outside of His love, and we should be exactly as He, in all respects. To Him, there are no untouchables, no one who cannot be absolved of sins— no matter how badly that one has behaved, when one sincerely turns from wickedness and seeks the ever-pure light.

———∞———

To know God as bliss, wisdom, light, expansiveness, and the deep—to know Him as our all and all, in all, is real freedom, true liberation.

———∞———

The Guru never ceases to see the perfect soul in God that each one of us truly are. Oh, such patience, a forbearance, that only God can display!

The savior parable is a description of a coming inner, spiritual illumination, for the striving devotee. New Jerusalem is a name for an enlightened state of consciousness and the predicted thousand years of peace is the same as the thousand petalled lotus—the spiritually illumined brain.

The promise of the spiritually illumined: this world is created out of the fabric of bliss, and it is also part and parcel of your innermost nature—it is yours to discover if you but make the effort to do so.

If joyful-bliss is a stranger to you, make it your business to recover it, for it absolutely exists deep in your Soul as your natural state.

Humility was His watchword, and though he spoke with great power and authority, still Jesus knew it is not I, but my Heavenly Father who does all things through me. In our quest to emulate Him, we too should manifest only the Father; let His light so shine through our thoughts, words, and actions, so that all will be inspired to seek out our Heavenly Father.

Jesus came in a line of perfect incarnations that our Heavenly Father has sent to show the way back to him. We error when we make a god of one of his incarnations and neglect the primary message that the same God that is in us is in him: God and the Kingdom of Heaven are to be found within us.

Yogacharya David seated at Sri Yukteswarji's
Samadhi Temple, Sermapore, India, 1999.

The Name Is Sweet

EXPANSION

Through Divine Communion, which must be constant, whatever is experienced is instantaneously purified. Through this method, purification can occur for individuals, groups of people, or for larger world conditions.

The main thing is to keep one's mind upon the Divine. Through constant God-remembrance the mind is purified and is lifted into the divine realms.

May the name of God ring out now and always, purifying hearts and minds everywhere, and leading all to the full realization of God.

When Nam (the name of God) is chanted with sincerity and full consciousness, a tremendous spiritual power is built. That power then goes out as a blessing to the world; so that what is done locally is felt globally. Any name of God is good; what is essential is the full faith and devotion of the chanter. Some of these names of God have been chanted for centuries, some for millennia.

I continue listening to the resounding Aum coming from everywhere and nowhere, and I know that it is the result of God's Presence combined with all the wonderful souls who celebrate this holy season, and this feeling, this music of Spirit, this is the best gift I could ever hope to receive. It is the vibrancy of the Holy Ghost and Christ Consciousness born anew, manifesting through this blissful sound. And its words sing through the very cells of my Being.

———

I quickly become indrawn, feeling the power of the chant in me and around me. A coursing energy flows from the back of my head, through my brain, and to a spot on my forehead. The mandir loses it physical bounds and expands into Spirit Omnipresent. Now bliss is flowing within and without; what is within, and what is without, loses all meaning.

———

It is God-experience alone that is the true Name of God: seeing the sacred Light, hearing the soaring AUM or AMEN, feeling the uplifting currents in the spine and brain, and expanding into infinite Spirit. Like a symphony orchestra, God can be the power of a violent storm or the sweetest touch of a spring breeze upon soft petals; God-experience encompasses all experience, and is far far beyond ordinary perception.

———

The Aum emanates from the creative principle from which all manifestation comes. The Amen originates from the Divine Consciousness, the Source of all that is. Listening to the Aum takes the mind back to its Source when deeply meditated upon.

This Aum/Amen is the Word, the Name of God. It is said that the Name of God and God are one. That is, by meditating upon this Name/Word, this inner sound, the mind dissolves and merges into the Divine Consciousness.

"Be still, and know that I am God" is your goal. Being still is not just sitting quietly; it requires that you empty the cup of your mind of all material concerns. You do this by shifting your attention to God-consciousness.

Being aware of your breath—you feel His peace. Thinking on God's name at the Christ Center—His light fills your Being. Going within—you inwardly hear His all-powerful voice as the Aum/Amen. Through expanding consciousness—you experience His bliss.

Your cup is sanctified, no longer polluted with fear, greed, and jealousy. You cannot hold it all and your cup runneth over—bliss, light, and the power of the Infinite pours out of your cup, flowing out in blessings to one and to all. Now the cup of your mind is completely still—His blissful Presence fills you without end.

The voice of God, resounding as the holy Aum/Amen, is heard through the inner ear, bringing a feeling of pressure at the back of my head. Just as the blissful feeling is not distinct to my spine only, so does the Aum/Amen expand out and out. This is a quality of spirit; it can be specific to a location, and it is also part of all-space; it can be as tiny as an atom or bigger than the universe—and it can be so simultaneously.

Then the light of God lights itself in the ajna. Initially, I see it as a bright star, then it illuminates the cranial cavity in a luminescent glow. Again, it defies being in a defined space, rather as the attention expands, so does the light. Awareness and light, awareness and sound, awareness and bliss merge and all are one—as awareness grows, so does the light, sound, and feeling of bliss, and those qualities of God-consciousness focuses or expand my awareness in whatever way they will, and in all of this, I am surrendered to what experience He chooses for me.

This experience is vastly superior to all sensory stimulations. It feels like home, and it makes a home of wherever I find myself. The intelligence and wisdom of God plays through my mind. All consciousness is instantly accessible. The thought that Lahiri Mahasaya's mahasamadhi and birthday are coming up at the end of this month flows through my awareness, and with it, a feeling of warmth and love sweeps over me.

Then I feel the master's mind transfer a thought into my own: I should make a diary note of my inner experiences today and make it a post. I submit to his request knowing that he will express through my receptivity.

The inner conscious contact with the supreme Being is simplicity itself.

We should practice faithfully, but not become overly focused on all the complexity of techniques and teachings—only go directly to the Source.

———✸———

The mountain of uplifted consciousness can be known through mystical experience; the ocean of expansive, unending Spirit you may have in deepened meditation; the purity of the clean desert vibration already exists for those who have eyes to see and ears to hear; and the prayag of two rivers becoming one happens right within you.

———✸———

You may know Divine Will initially as the spiritual practice prescribed for you: meditate morning and night, chant His holy name, practice seeing Him as all in all, be in service to Him in all forms you meet, love Him more than you love the world, and always tell the truth. As you practice these ways with sincerity, an inner life awakens inside of you. Sporadically at first, then continually you know the Divine guidance and Presence through your purified mind—a result of your spiritual practice and Grace.

———✸———

There are certain names of God—in all languages—that have been surcharged through sacred repetition that has lifted up saints into the highest Consciousness, like a trail that has been blazed through the wilderness by thousands of years and thousands of feet that wear even sharp stones to smoothness.

"Ram Nam" auspiciously qualifies as one of the most ancient and well used of such incantations.

———

Ram Nam practice takes the aspirant through a number of stages. From the beginning, chanting Ram Nam has given me a feeling of upliftment, peace, and bliss. This purification results in continuous God-experience—feeling His presence permeating mind, body, and spirit. At a certain point, the vibration of Ram Nam enters the spine, awakening an awareness of vast inner space filled with sacredness. The illumined spine and brain then effortlessly merges with outer creation—God within, God without. This universal vision confirms that there is no place where God is not.

———

As we have circumambulated this remarkable North American Continent, we have chanted God's Name as part of this spiritual pilgrimage. While moving down the road, I feel the spiritual aura radiating out through the power of the name (Nam) as a gift from the Infinite—awakening and resonating with the Divine vibration underlying all creation. God alone knows the full purpose of our pilgrimage, but the power of God's Name is definitely a part of it.

The holy mantra "Om Sri Ram Jai Ram Jai Jai Ram." is imbued with an all-powerful uplifting Grace. With God's name ever being chanted, the transformed consciousness of those who attain spiritual heights through the Nam further surcharges it with ever greater and greater power to help others do the same.

Imagine the vibration of many devotees chanting this holy mantra in full devotion towards the Infinite—helping to raise the consciousness of this world and all its inhabitants. The Lord knows this world is in need of upliftment, and though we may be in disparate places, we are all in union with our infinite Beloved through chanting and harmonizing with His Holy Nam.

We celebrate Good Friday, singing blissful songs of praise for the coming of the Christ (Consciousness). This feeling of upliftment, and the intimacy of the Last Supper, are preludes to the most difficult time to come: the Mystical Crucifixion. Consciousness along the spine (the twelve disciples) thrills at the joyous response of Jerusalem (higher consciousness of the brain), but the all-knowing Christ is aware of what is to follow. And you, as you share in the bliss of upliftment will think, like the disciples, "This bliss will never end."

However, the time of testing and purification will commence at its appointed time. With this test comes solace in the promise of the Christ, "Lo, I am with you always." And so He is, even though you may not always be conscious of this fact. Do not fear, God guides, and His direction is correct and true. Do not hold back—go on boldly—knowing that though your humanness dies when it is mystically crucified, the eternal Christ Consciousness is resurrected in you for all time.

———∞———

The universal cathedral of God occurs when the love of God, by whatever name (or no name) He or She is called, is broad enough to include all humankind and is made manifest here on earth as the universal vision in which all are known to be various expressions of the one Supreme Spirit.

———∞———

Spiritual freedom and purity are vastly superior to anything the five senses can offer. The body uses divine power and directs it through the nerves; when channeled through the senses, you are experiencing pure spiritual energy indirectly, and much diluted. However, when you have God-experience, you tap directly into the Source of the intelligence and power that is creating this entire universe.

You may think of the yogis sitting in their caves in deep meditation as the ones who are doing without—sitting all alone and nothing interesting happens. In reality, they are united with the kingdom of heaven that is all bliss, fulfillment, and knowledge of God—they are monarchs not of this earth, but of infinite Spirit. By comparison, this earth in a carnal sense, will seem grubby, shabby, and low grade.

———∞———

From Buddha and Jesus, we have examples of loving compassion as a hallmark of their lives and teachings. Looking
at the world through their eyes, we see all humanity,
nay, all creation, as intimately connected with our own
existence; their welfare is not separate from ours. Papa
Ramdas embodied this universal vision, and Master and
Mother gave the love of God to one and all. Surely, the
world has had teachings and examples enough for us to
know what is right and wrong, yet human nature periodically wants to exert itself to dominate over its brothers
and sisters to not lift them up.

Remember, nothing is done in secret that will not be
shouted from the rooftops! Let us be our brother's and
our sister's keepers and support one another, bring out
the best in one another. Our time here is short, but we
are accountable for what we do, so let us do right at all
times and in all places; and more than that, see all others
in their true essence, as beings of Divine origins, and to
be respected as such.

There is no greater power in all of creation than love; it
makes you want to be absorbed in your Beloved and lose
yourself in Him.

The angel Gabriel is sounding his trumpet, calling all to
the revelatory altar of the one true living God—this "Call"

reverberates across space, and opens wide the way for truth. Yes, there will be false prophets along the way; that is inevitable. However, there will also be true God-men and God-women who will bless this earth and all humankind, who will reveal the truth and awaken other men and women across the globe, bringing this world into higher states of illumination.

There is no limit to this transformation. It all starts with those who are responsive to the call of the truth and with those who have the courage to seek it out.

———

Just think of a world in which each person serves all others with love—what a tremendous world that will be!

———

To meditate deeply, to serve the Infinite in all one does, to commit to using discrimination and making God first, and to love the Beloved with all one's heart, is to draw nigh to blessed Spirit.

———

Besides the relatively thin layer of the subconscious mind, there is the vast superconscious mind—not usually directly perceived by the conscious mind. When the superconscious mind illumines the conscious mind, it brings inspiration, intuitive flashes of truth, a higher order of Reality that supersedes both the normal waking conscious mind and the oftentimes murky depths of the subconscious mind.

Throughout the "Dark Night of the Soul" that God and Guru put me through, I somehow knew that it was Divine Will that was at work.

To breathe, open, and allow your Divine Friend, Guide and Savior to gain entry into your innermost pain and aloneness means that you are on the pathway to wholeness, that you are growing in God—merging into Him even as He is merging into you.

In Kriya, our life-force moves in a circuit through our spine and brain; in Hong-Sau and Ram Nam our mind is focused on the mantra. The result: our breathing is significantly slowed, we feel a release of tension from our body, and we enter into a quiet zone that not only slows our breathing, but our thinking transforms into pure witness awareness—we become the observer of all that is. A deeper breath, an even bigger release of tension, and we enjoy surpassingly beautiful peace; the joy of Spirit bubbles up from a deep Source in us and we feel expansive— our system is now being rebooted.

To become still is the goal of Kriya Yoga and its after-effect. The chanting of God's name is meant to result in that same stillness.

To be established in inner stillness brings about the extraordinary state of oneness.

With deepened practice, we can touch that realm of inner silence that gives us true rest.

We practice our kriya, chant God's name, meditate on Hong Sau, and suddenly we find ourselves dropping into that inner realm of stillness—even if for a moment.

———∞———

"Tyranny, like hell, is not easily conquered; yet we have this consolation with us, that the harder the conflict, the more glorious the triumph."[8] When you conquer hell by realizing God, the glory of triumph is not a tickertape parade, or your picture in the paper, but it is the bliss that wells up from deep within; it is the Light of your eternal Being blazing, and it is the revelations of inspired wisdom from the Infinite.

Anchor yourself in this thought in times of crises and in times of ease: God, gurus, and all the saints and spiritual masters who have ever tread this path of realization are with me. Awareness of the fact that I never stand alone means that when I touch the fabric of God's Being through remembrance of Him, I touch the glory of all that He is!

———∞———

Our spiritual practice bears the fruit of bliss, light, and universal love on our tree of consciousness.

———∞———

---

8   A Thomas Paine quote: https://www.goodreads.com/quotes/36115-tyranny-like-hell-is-not-easily-conquered-yet-we-have

Learn to touch upon the power of stillness; make it a part
of a daily practice.

———❧———

What makes us know we are making progress? It is the
increasing spiritual freedom we experience even when
discharging our worldly duties. Whether it is running a
company, or washing the dishes, we feel God's Presence
with us—His strength, joy, and wisdom, flowing through
us at all times. The family home is our ashram, and just
like a monk's ashram, the everyday chores must still be
done: food selected and lovingly prepared, work that supplies the needs for food, arranged shelter, and much more.

We must work through the rough edges of interrela-
tionships that rub up against one another. Our home is
our ashram, and what makes it so is our love, dedication,
and surrender to God.

———❧———

Find the calm center. This requires real spiritual practice.
In moments during meditation, you find it, then it begins
to generalize to when you are participating fully in the
world. At such times, a sudden feeling of peace fills you,
and you realize, "This is one of those magic-moments."
Love fills your heart and overflows to all the world. At
such times as these, you touch the hem of God—fears
and craving-desires subside—life is perfect.

———❧———

The advanced practitioner may instantly phase out of the
physical body and phase into the spiritual. Here, the limits

of the three bodies no longer pertain; rather, there is an expansive freedom in which even an idea is limiting.

This freedom is pervaded by a feeling of purity, and while thought is transcended, awareness is very much intact. In this purity is a sublime exaltation—bliss is all-pervasive. So, expansiveness, purity, bliss, and pure awareness are the realities of this spiritual state of being or God-consciousness.

The spiritual man, or woman, can transition through the physical, astral, or causal bodies and enter a spiritual state of Being that is beyond all three lower bodies.

Bliss is a most interesting phenomenon. It is always identifiable as bliss, a common signature that you know it when you experience it. Yet, within that unity it is constantly changing, ever-new. By continued practice of meditation, you may be aware of the life-energy in either a static form, as your astral body, or kinetic motion. As an astral body, you are filled with a wonderful, vibrating hum of life-energy units, or life-trons, that make up your astral form. Consistent with life-energy, creating a form or a body, it also flows directionally or multi-directionally. This life-tron, or prana, is responsive to your will, and also has an intelligence of its own that can dictate what it does and where it goes.

From the perspective of a few steps removed, those decisions, actions, and revelations create pictures that illumine
His plan. Even those things I thought were mistakes at the
time all add up to something beautiful for God. When
mistakes equal learning, and learning produces growth,
then even what does harm in the moment can be made
to serve a higher good in the end—those crazy dots not
only make the picture interesting, but the darkish shadows make the brightness all the more brilliant.

I remember being at the Van Gogh Museum in Amsterdam.
A guide explained how his pictures are made up of so
many tiny dots. When you stand close to the painting,
you see many, many fine colored points that do not really
make sense. Then, as you take steps away from the picture, those dots begin to coalesce into flowers, rivers,
trees, and reflections in water—it all comes together into
a beautiful portrait. Who could have known this when
seeing only tiny strokes of color up close? In this way,
we may see our lives as so many little actions and decisions throughout the day. Those little decisions may seem
insignificant on their own but without those tiny dots of
action, there would be no larger picture when we step
back to see what has been created.

Look forward to the future, do not project a bad year
onto the new one. We have a blank canvas upon which to
paint, an empty book with fresh pages to write upon. Sri

Yukteswarji said that God creates this universe; he did not say God created, but God creates. We are co-creating our life with God. We are in a constant state of becoming, and each moment holds the potential for all eternity in it.

Your challenge is to be clear with your purpose and to be exactly on track with achieving it. So that when it comes time to draw your last breath, you feel in perfect accord with Divine Will, and can, in all good conscience, commend yourself to the highest light of your Being—that is what the Infinite has desired for you from the foundation of time.

If someone is struggling with staying true to his or her higher Self, then, through an omnipresent state of witnessing, they can, if discerning, sense the future consequences of wrong action, as can we on their behalf. We see the future consequences of wrong actions, and know all of the suffering that individual will go through; our heart goes out to such a one even as they fall short of the goal.

It is human nature to be attracted to that which is pleasurable and be repulsed by that which causes pain, so to appreciate that all is God, our experience must rise above the two forces of attraction and repulsion. In order to do that, we must experience a higher order of consciousness; our consciousness must rise to the level of

God-consciousness in which all creation is seen as Divine. Anything less leaves us in the dual realm and entails suffering. This suffering is different than body pain; it is suffering of consciousness because we feel separated from God.

—— ∞ ——

When we are in need, we increase our prayer-demand that He give us more, and we open wider to the idea that we are His instrument. A loving father may test his child in order that he or she learns an important lesson, but a loving parent would never abandon a child; so, our Heavenly Father, Divine Mother may test us to hone our focus of attention to be upon God alone.

—— ∞ ——

To feel God weaving Himself through every experience you have in life and to know that it is He alone who exists; One without a second. Why should you suffer separation for one moment longer? There is no reason. He is calling you with His divine magnetism, for it is He, it is He, it is all He; there is nothing else. So, be that! It can all start with chanting His holy Name: Om Sri Ram Jai Ram Jai Jai Ram; Victory to God, Victory to the Light.

—— ∞ ——

Keep that openness to the infinite supply of Spirit.

—— ∞ ——

HEALTH

"Why then," you may ask, "is there a physical problem when God is present?" There are many times when God's Presence can and does manifest as complete physical healing. However, there are a variety of causes that manifest as physical problems, and there are times when God will use His physical instruments to fulfill His higher will. Thus, there is no contradiction in His perfection and His use of a physical body to fulfill a necessary karma, or bring about desirable outcomes on this earth. As Jesus said, "This sickness will not end in death but is for the glory of God" (John 11:4).

———

Anchor directly and permanently to perfect health through God-tuned thought.

———

Prana, coming from God, is nothing but God in that form—to practice allowing the pain impulse to pass through the brain and into the light, not simply to be absorbed in the brain, affirming that the life-energy in this form is God, just as all other forms of life-energy are God.

———

Whether it is a short meditational restart or a deeper complete shutdown, let us look for the signs that make us know we have had a successful reboot. Then we will maximize the body-mind workstation and wonderfully synchronize with God's Mainframe Divine Consciousness.

———

The body's hardware can also get stuck in repeating cycles: tense muscles in the neck, jaw, eyes, back—well, anywhere you have muscles, they can become tense and remain that way. Your blood pressure gets higher, digestive secretions secrete way too much—there are so many ways for the body-hardware to malfunction, resulting in power drains, bloatware clogging, and inflammation in the operating systems, even leading to catastrophic body failures.

———

Our bodies are working miracles and right nutrition, right thinking, and God can heal what ails the body.

———

Life-force, or Prana, is the underlying cause of healing as it works through the cells and our intelligence.

———

Master gave us a gift through his Energization Exercises: practice tensing and releasing and feeling the life-force flowing into body parts.

———

The Alternate Nostril Breathing practice has a calming effect along with improving the ability to focus the mind.

It is amazing how much abuse our body can take. Perhaps that is not always to our benefit because we start to think it doesn't make any difference how we treat it. However, unhealthy patterns tend to have a cumulative effect and when our body gives us trouble, we feel betrayed; the real betrayal usually occurred many years before, based on how we fed and treated the body.

Remember, food is not only the fuel our body needs, but it is also the original pharmacy for healing and keeping our body well.

Hippocrates said, let your medicine be food, and your food medicine. Life lesson: Let all the activities of your body, mind, and spirit be what is best and for the highest in you, and through the law of cause and effect, good things will come to you.

Investigate the marvelous ways in which the body has been constructed—I mean, truly amazing intelligence that has gone into its design—and then how little thought is given to feeding it high quality fuel and providing what it needs for optimum living. Show gratitude to your Creator for the miraculous gift He has bestowed upon you. It is high time to show that appreciation, starting today, by living with healthy habits and honoring this amazing Temple.

Look to the highest quality in every part of your life. You are building a perfect house in God every day of your life. The materials you choose and the care with which you build both increases your satisfaction today and will make a vast difference in your life and the lives of all those you touch as time unfolds.

Create with the uplifting quality of God in all you do and experience the difference.

LOVE AND TRUTH

The Divine Presence in you now naturally radiates out of you to uplift and heal creation of its suffering.

We all broadcast what we experience in life to those whom our lives touch. Being in tune with the Divine Presence increases the power of what you transmit, bringing solace, beauty, and purity to this world.

God uses you to broadcast His love and compassion to all creation! There is truly nothing more useful or deeply meaningful for you than to lead a life of true Self-interest.

Practice chanting the all-powerful name of God when in social situations. See the light radiating from your own heart and surrounding those who are around you. Feel the freedom this invokes within you, and you will see it has its effect on others as well. Those who are obstacles to this practice are in your life to make you stronger.

Self-mastery teaches you that when you put God first, you will find a peaceful bliss that the world simply cannot give to you—and that universal love will be the hallmark of your life.

When every cell of your being resonates with divine feeling, you may be sure you are in God-consciousness. You know that you are not the body, not any temporary emotional state, and you are beyond thought—you are eternal Spirit existing in a state of freedom. The power of chanting is becoming more widely known, but what a power it unleashes to lift one and all into the bliss of His Presence—through continuous and earnest practice, He must come to you.

———

To listen and learn, a most perfect message. Ah, learning to listen to God, what a day that is when you open the door and really attune yourself to what God is speaking to you. And, what an attentive friend and lover God is: infinite in knowledge and wisdom, full of fun and joy, a constant life-stream coming through the medulla, a guiding light at the ajna, unfolding into infinite reaches from the crown chakra—there is nothing in the world that can compare!

———

A morning thought came streaming through with the sun, hammering away the walls of darkness and separation; this thought was a powerful tool for breaking duality's hold on the mind.

———

The master proclaims that stones also sing the name of God—perhaps even more readily than sophisticated humans?

———

The price of entry for discovering this here-and-now reward of spiritual attributes is, of course, to keep our mind on God: to breathe, be a mindful witness to all experiences, to keep our attention at the ajna (point between the eyebrows), to chant His name, and to meditate deeply upon Him.

Love is the most powerful attractor in this world and beyond. Love of God automatically brings about detachment. Love of God is the most powerful asset for living in the world, but not being of it.

———

The "software of your mind" can get stuck in a continuous loop. Thinking, thinking, thinking, always thinking on some topic, some obsession, some object of desire or fear, or simply an endless loop of a commercial jingle you heard (if you have ever been on Disneyland's ride "It's a Small World," then you will have been subjected to this kind of diabolical jingle/abuse programming!) Anytime such a tune gets going in my head, I sing Ram Nam to the tune to be deprogrammed. It almost always breaks the cyclic nature of the tune, and even if it doesn't, I am still continuously singing the Name of God.

———

How remarkable when the life and teachings of Jesus the Christ jumps off the pages from ancient texts and awakens a sleeping God-hood within.

———

True spiritual experience brings unsurpassed peace, inner assurance, expanding bliss, a knowledge of who and what you truly are, an intuitive understanding and realization that only comes with upliftment in consciousness.

———

Chanting is unparalleled for keeping the mind on God and feeling His Bliss.

———

When there is only God, and God is love, then how can we do anything but love all—even as God does.

———

God gives us lessons to free us from the uncertainties of life in the body, and to anchor us in His supreme state of Consciousness. He untangles our attachment to this body and makes us focus on His sacred love and upliftment.

———

SEARCHING

The simplest means to have non-attachment is to have a total focus on, and surrender to, God—by making Him first in your heart, mind, and soul. Be a faithful lover of God: chant His name all the hours of the day, feel His bliss surging throughout your entire being, and you will be His, and He will be yours.

Non-attachment to this world and perfect comprehension of the universal vision of God make for pure happiness no matter your situation.

⸎

Find the sweetness of the Divine Name singing itself in your heart, mind, and soul.

⸎

There is a way of inwardly listening to the vibrational consciousness of a place by being quiet and receptive. Too much concern with schedules, other people around you, and other distractions, and you will miss what a place has to say to you.

⸎

God meant this life to be lived in joy and light. The fact that we have wandered away from this vision of a Divine Life does not mean we are to be forsaken. Divine Mother is calling us to be awake to the fact that this creation is sacred, holy ground, and Heavenly Father wants us to know that there is a sure, unflappable, source of peace and inner assurance that transcends the thralldom of duality.

The healing of the fissure between heaven and hell is as close as our next thought; simply lay the healing balm of God-remembrance upon the past, present, and anticipated future.

Papa said that when he left to go on train and foot all over India, it was because God wanted to demonstrate that He is universally present. And although I have ventured to many parts of the world, there are many areas of America yet to see. It seems that God is out to demonstrate that He truly is equally present in all places and people of America. In addition, it has given us a chance to chant His holy name wherever we go, adding our part of God to all the people and places to which we have traveled.

As Papa said so truly, you do not need to leave hearth and home to practice God-remembrance. To make your life a sacred journey, regard each and every aspect of it as steps to your full realization—the attainment of your life's greatest aim.

Sacred imagery is always pointing to the supreme Reality. However, when the story is taken only at its face value, the mind becomes fixated on the fascinating but bewildering outer images of the parable.

Ask yourself, "Do I feel ever-new joy? Is there peace and an inner stillness at the core of who I am and what I do? Is the Divine Presence with me day and night? Are my thoughts, words, and actions worthy of being a child of the Infinite?" These hallmarks are indications of true spiritual growth and let us know when we are making progress.

The importance of finding joy in life cannot be fully fathomed in a day, a month, or even a lifetime. This is due to the fact that joyful-bliss is part and parcel of God's Being.

The name of God in India is Sat-Chid-Ananda, and the last, Ananda, means Bliss. It is one of the eternal verities of the Infinite.

Revelations and insights to Spiritual Truth date back to our earliest records. Stories told around the campfire, initiation ceremonies, quests for higher visions, systems of thought, and methods for transformation find expression in simple and remarkably complex ways. Wherever we look in this wide world, we can gather evidence of humans seeking higher understanding from the dawn of humankind.

The Indus River Valley has statues of meditators from three thousand B.C. Ancient Egypt, Babylonia, Persia, China, the Pueblos, Incas and Mayans all display theologies, architecture, poetry, art and stories that are part of a rich history of humankind's pursuit for higher knowledge. There is something in human beings that is innately drawn to understand that which goes beyond the five senses.

Amongst many societies theological exploration gave meaning to acts of nature, helped to heal the sick, forecast the future, and spoke to the ultimate mystery—death. Worldwide there has been the recognition of entities beyond the physical realm: ghosts, angels, and gods. And ultimately, there was the realization of a singular ruling intelligence and power: God. God stood beyond normal conceptions of relative worldly powers, supernatural powers, and god-like personalities. Recognition of God, something that was beyond description, circumscription, absent even a form, was understood by at least a few superior men and women. Even in systems of thought that talked of higher beings such as angels and gods there was knowledge of God as the "beyond the beyond."

At any one time there were minds able to grasp this wisdom and give expression to it through words, stories, and artistic expression. Others of lesser intelligence and realization naturally followed in the footsteps of towering spiritual personalities, but failed to fully comprehend the supreme Truth: these lesser ones formed movements or organizations, aligned with political powers, often to the aggrandizement of the ego, and created stable structures of religious institutions. To the degree the original Truth was taught there was much good, but there were also distortions, falsehoods, and evil that came from misrepresentations and ignorance of the Truth.

For the propagation of teachings, a structure most often arises, but with structure comes those attracted more by name and fame, power and prestige, and in this type of structural organization what is too often sacrificed is the Truth. Creating a balance between the tension of intuitively derived revelations and the structure to hold Truth has been the story of the great religions. There have been spiritual masters who have left disciples, oral and written teachings as their legacy, and others have simply faded into the Infinite with barely a trace in the material world. There are some who are remembered by the world, but not by God; others who vanish to the world but are great in the mind of God, and a few who are honored by both by the world and by God.

Jesus of Nazareth (who became known as the Christ, the anointed One, the Messiah), is of this last category. The world reveres what it knows of his life as portrayed by a few of his direct disciples and others who followed in the footsteps of direct disciples. Not only does the world honor his name, but he was glorified by his heavenly Father, "This is my Son, in whom I am well pleased."

As we enter into this upward swing of the Dwapara Yuga there is a greater degree of personal choice; with higher highs and lower lows. Each of us is in a position to decide what it all means on a personal level to follow, or not to follow, the master. With the teachings of Paramhansa Yogananda and Mother Hamilton we have the unique privilege of a remarkable treasure trove of teachings that knowledge of history, language study, and theology alone cannot reveal. As Mother Hamilton said, she paid the Pearl of Great Price for the Truth she brought forth from the scriptures. I want you to focus on the meaning of Jesus' life for yourself. Experiential spirituality means God is awake within you and leading you toward your oneness with this matchless state of Being. Becoming a Christ-ian, as Mother said it, means this fiery initiation into Christ Consciousness will touch every facet of your life; it is a total makeover from the human to the Divine. This is what it means to follow Jesus, even to the death of your ego-self, so that the Divine within you may be resurrected.

The Life and Teachings of Jesus echo down the ages and are flaming words of Truth that are empowered to set you free when you dive deep in meditation, touching the power and majesty of your eternal God-nature. [9]

---

9   Excerpt adapted from Yogacharya David's *Christian Yoga* chapter titled The Way of the Cross and the Christ.

Yogacharya David at top of ridge in Utah mountains, 2018.

Who is the Self?

GOD'S DESIGN

True silence makes the consciousness expand. Whether we are viewing life across an open expanse of desert, from a high mountain top, over a vast body of water, or from our "yogi's cave" in our home, stillness makes it easy for our mind to lose it bounds and seek out vastness. Master Mahasaya said his great guru, Sri Ramakrishna, told him to always meditate when he was next to a body of water in order to go beyond body consciousness.

Once remembered, Spirit's domain in eternity does not easily accommodate the small confines of a human body or ego-consciousness. When we seek out the attributes of God, we yearn for freedom, peace, joy, love, and knowing who and what we truly are—pristine nature can help us realize this impulse.

Our Soul is in inseparable union with God as His likeness—this union is pure bliss, unalloyed joy, a conscious realization of our oneness with the infinite, eternal Reality.

We do spiritual practice in order to re-member, bring back together that which is seemingly separate.

The ultimate truth is that humankind is, and ever has been, an expression of God; we are made in His image. However, we have a veil of ignorance, drawn like a curtain, that makes us believe we are forever separate.

———&———

Your life is "right-sized" for you; you need only open yourself to all that God wishes to manifest through you.

———&———

Share in this God-experience. You will find it waiting for you to unwrap from under your tree-of-life, right within you.

———&———

Any time you are feeling too cramped in your living space, feeling the pressure of life, and that you are too small for the shoes you are wearing, then, instantly, recall who and what you truly are—a child of the Infinite—as such, you expand to be larger than the problems and challenges you face; you walk amongst the stars and that vast resources are streaming to you in order for you to live your life exactly as it has been ordered from above.

———&———

There is plenty of room for you to breathe, live your life, and be exactly who God designed you to be.

———&———

When meditating, bring to mind your expansiveness. Feel that you are not limited to one little human body; rather, know yourself to be a citizen of the stars, that there is no limit to consciousness. When done with meditation time and you reenter into the world, continue your connection with your greater Self—that you are a living instrument of limitless thought, energy, and abundance.

Even a glimpse of the beauty and transcendence of the superconscious mind can inspire life to new heights; it awakens our awareness to a new way of experiencing life; it is the doorway to the vast ocean that creates the waves of creation on the surface; but oh, it is so much more.

The superconscious mind—this under-the-wave Reality is blissful, enlightening, and leads to the supreme truth. The alternating waves of this material reality fade into a shadowy twilight compared to the rising dawn that reveals a bright and beautiful world all around.

The astounded conscious mind discovers that this Reality has always been with us, only the ordinary mind simply did not have the light to see it.

The Buddha is a title that means the "Awakened One," having the same meaning as the title, the Christ, "The Anointed One." It denotes the one who is awake to this greater superconscious reality—the one who sees it through newly awakened eyes gains new understanding and develops a new awareness.

———∞∞∞———

True stillness takes us beyond ourselves; stillness is the gateway to realizing our oneness with the Infinite.

———∞∞∞———

To uncover the greater reality is our spiritual journey, for this higher truth is what is called spirituality. To do this, we must open new ways of perceiving ourselves and this world.

———∞∞∞———

As concentration advances in meditation practice, one becomes aware of the idea plane of consciousness. Here, deep concentration takes the practitioner beyond the physical preoccupations of this world, and beyond the energy-astral body.

———∞∞∞———

It is the Supreme Consciousness that dwells in you and all through you. This realization makes you truly free, fulfilled, and aware of His divine Presence and Bliss coursing throughout your Being, day and night.

———∞∞∞———

Let us close our eyes, go within, and discover sacred life-force flowing throughout our being; then our divine awareness can expand out to the furthest reaches of space. With the inner sight awakened, we open our two eyes and we comprehend the same sacred force operating through all of nature, in all of humanity, in every living thing in space.

We have awakened to Christ Consciousness, we have ascended and, in seeing this, we know the Heavenly Father—we realize, "I am That."

Once we have had an experience in transcendent consciousness, we will feel that before we were sleepwalking in life. It is as if the scales fall from our eyes, and we see inner and outer reality in a brand-new way.

Right action, or dharma, is the most efficient means forward, both in this world and spiritually. While wrong action can look more expedient in the moment, it inevitably builds resistant karma that immediately, or eventually, causes suffering, and undermines success.

Feel the indistinct boundaries around you dissolve and expand out into an ocean of bliss and purity of Spirit—centered everywhere, circumferenced nowhere.

The veil of maya can lower like a curtain and make us believe there is only so much, and not more. In our response, we let that limitation arouse in us unlimited

Spirit. It is then that we have set ourselves a new course with open-ended potential. It is true we may find that we are immediately surrounded by limitations. But each limitation can only arouse greater focus on God, Light, Love, and Intelligence.

We need a determined will to propel us to seek out and consciously connect with the Creator of all that we see, and much, much more; then, we take the first steps to free ourselves of the tyranny of human-made limits.

—⊗⊗⊗—

Each soul is a transmitting and receiving station, and through communion with Divine Consciousness may transmit powerful spiritual vibrations, such as love and light, out to particular souls that come to mind, or various groups, or creation itself.

—⊗⊗⊗—

PURUSHA AND PRAKRITI

The angels' universal sound is singing its song in my ears and beyond; the warm Christ-light is blazing as the leading star and it lights the Christmas tree of my spine and brain, and love is glowing from my heart, radiating out to all creation. These thought-feelings fill my heart, mind, and soul, and I share them with one and all— there is no limit, no aloneness, no feeling of loss possible in this ever-new birth.

———

Christ Consciousness resurrects union with God beyond the duality of good and evil.

———

I stand on the brink of timelessness, and from that perspective, I am, and we are all, eternally at the beginning. It is exciting, enthralling, and propelling to think of all that can be explored, all the ways we might serve—everything that God has for each one of us, as His life unfolds before us.

———

It is true that a God-man or a God-woman has access to extraordinary power and consciousness, however, that one still lives in a human body, faces many of the same trials that any human being does, and can even feel despondent.

The reality of each and every moment is a crux—a crucial space in time that holds infinite possibilities. It is only a habit of mind that makes us focus on a narrow spectrum of reality, that makes us think that we and our world are not touched by a transcendent beauty, power, and intelligence.

By making conscious contact with infinite Reality, we open an access to so much more than what we ordinarily think of as self. By claiming this higher Reality as our own, we become new, whole.

Creativity, makes things happen, brings in new ideas, and awakens the feeling of God and the sacredness of life; all these are products of life-energy. Everyone has some gift of this life-force to offer this world—some to a wider extent, others in a quieter way. We can feel this life-force energy in ourselves and others.

After being in a high state of meditation for some time and enjoying bliss, a thought may come from that highest consciousness. Only now, the thought does not create restlessness; rather, the thought is in perfect harmony with highest divinity. From this thought, life-energy may flow as creation, and thought and life-energy may move through the physical body. In all three bodies there is a knowing connection that comes from the highest state of consciousness—a phasing in of the spiritual still-state of the highest consciousness that expresses itself in one, two, or three of the lower bodies. The eyes open, and the same astral, causal, and spiritual states are now all seen as manifesting in the world as all there is—God is known to be all-pervading.

<hr>

For God is the seed-force in one and in all. In truth, God is the driving power behind everything we think, say, and do, whether it be mundane or spiritual. For, everything in our life is orchestrating events so that we might come to our ultimate hero's journey.

<hr>

This world is full of divisions. However, underlying all divisions there beats the unifying rhythm of bliss that ties everything together in perfect harmony.

<hr>

Gradually, we are permanently established in The Deep. Now, worldly-experience is seen as passing phenomenon yet we never exclusively identify with it. We realize that The Deep is our true Self, and that we are ever That.

<hr>

Let us be forever one in Him, merged in His bliss and comfort, no matter what dance steps are being taught by our Infinite Beloved.

<hr>

What a beguiling Lover God is; the world generally goes by without a second thought for the "Fulfiller of our heart's desires." Rather, we lead lives of "quiet desperation," not truly ourselves or what we are meant to be. Try to convince a worldly man or woman of the extraordinary potential they carry within. They do not have the eyes to see nor the ears to hear.

―――◦◦◦◦―――

There is a power, a pulsation that runs through all creation. When you awaken to the Divine Life your awareness of this power grows. To know its true nature, requires a stillness within.

―――◦◦◦◦―――

Create a listening heart and mind that is not consumed with the senses and worldly preoccupations. When you touch the higher realms, you are being exposed to the raw data that has formed this universe, not someone's interpretation of how they say it is.

―――◦◦◦◦―――

As God creates all there is, He says, "It is good." Therefore, God (as the supreme Good) is the same whether She is the expressive Power, or as the supreme Spirit beyond creation. We need only be mindful that we are Mini-Me's of God, and not lose touch with who and what we really are in all circumstances.

―――◦◦◦◦―――

I sit in inner stillness; a tremendous pressure is in the base of my skull. I focus inside this intense pain; the sound of Aum/Amen is remarkably loud. My vision goes into the center of this dense power; I see the "atoms" inside this density, what appears to me now as so many galaxies in a vast universe. The compact density expands, the pressure in my head reduces, and the feeling of power increases, only now it is spread out over vast space.

There is so much power behind creation, inside the cell, an atom, and even a quark; it is all the power of creation itself. Dumb power could not create out of randomness all that we see about us. I perceive the great intelligence and beauty in this power; to perceive this vision is awe-inspiring.

This mystical experience is the remover of fear and the birth of Christ Consciousness. The microcosm and the macrocosm are not different but are expressions of the one power. This is a mystery to the uninitiated, and self-evident to those who know.

The holy birth is here, it is now, and it is ever-present.

There is one compelling reason for knowing God—it is only through oneness with Him that we can have lasting happiness, a fulfillment that does not diminish with time nor is severed by death.

With all realized Beings—each one has a unique expression. When the personality has been subsumed in Divine

Consciousness, if it is the Divine Will, that one is reborn, so to speak, as a Divine personality for the benefit of the world. One of the great lessons you learn in having a pantheon of a guru-lineage and coming into close association with saints is that you do not have to become an imitation of the personality of a God-realized individual; rather, you learn what is essential to all God-realized beings.

———⊗⊗⊗———

Remain anchored to the Divine: experience yourselves to be the vast ocean of consciousness underneath the ever-changing waves—the alternations of being happy and sad only play on the surface, never touching your deeper Self.

———⊗⊗⊗———

It has also been interesting to note in this exploration of God's great body that, even in realizing God as the indwelling Presence, and knowing He is with me always, there are still variations in spiritual power in this place versus that, or in one person more than another.

So, while God is known as the eternal Self within, and He is to be found in all creation as its Creator and Sustainer, and in truth, it is He who manifests Himself as all there is; still, the vibration of Spirit in creation comes in different hues, colors, and strength throughout His vast expression.

———⊗⊗⊗———

"I AM"

I can tell you beloved friend, the great "I Am" answers all of the heart's desires, it fulfills the soul and its constant restless tides, and it is easily accessible by all. Oh, my dear ones, simply make no qualification upon God or His creation, humbly accept everything in its perfection, merge into the great "I Am", and join Lahiri Baba and the great ones in knowing this fathomless Truth of your Being.

⸻

In fact, how can we say that any in the world are strangers? Are not all our intimates? If there is suffering by anyone, is it not our very self that is also suffering? This universal empathy would not be possible without the Presence of God in the midst, for it would overwhelm the individual mind. However, the universal mind of God can easily accommodate this expansion.

⸻

Let us so transform our lives that we feel that we are living as kindred spirits with all the great spiritual masters. Mother felt that Master was so great that he was Christ come again. Boldly dare to claim your kinship with these greatest masters. Be inspired by Master's life and example, and know the greatest open secret in all the world.

⸻

Contacting God is youthfulness itself. The Self is always youthful in spirit.

A secret: realizing God will satisfy your heart, completely.

God is dwelling in your heart right in this moment.

The moral of the story, the story of your existence; all that you treasure, all that you hold dear is right within you, within your heart, mind, and soul. And even if the instruments of body and mind were to become broken or destroyed, your Soul, the repository of your entire existence will forever know those experiences.

The love you have experienced, the joy you have known, the security that made you feel whole, all of that and more are elements of who you really are and have always been.

The sword is in Krishna's hand, and while I am here, I will sing, and dance, and serve, and be in the joy of God for all the days of my life.

Do not lose connection with that vast aspect of yourself that is beneath the surface—your greater qualities. Bring the bliss of His presence into your heart and soul so that heaven and earth may merge and become as one.

Meditating upon the great "I AM," chanting His name, surrendering to His will, and immersing yourself in the bliss of God will purge you of every limitation and liberate you in full spiritual realization so that you will never be entrapped in ignorance again—this is the endgame in the practice of positive tapas.

Keep your mind lovingly focused on God and surrendered to His will, it is the most positive, easiest, and the most direct way to immerse yourself in God-experience.

———

This is humankind's next evolutionary step; and it occurs within the devoted individual, and as more individuals burst the shell of humanness, a forest of Christ-like souls will inhabit this earth—bringing a new era of peace and fulfilling mankind's greatest potential.

———

In my journey to God, He has given me direct spontaneous memories of previous lives: the capacity to fully relive them just as they occurred. One such life memory included dying and what happened immediately after. In that moment of separation from the body, which came as an immense relief, I found myself in the presence of a wonderful Being of Light. Mother explained that this was my own Christ-Self—the God within me made manifest in this seemingly outer form. Together, we reviewed my life with an eye for learning, this Light-form communicated through thought-transference, conveyed insight, wisdom, and compassion.

We are married to the Beloved, and in all situations our Heavenly Father and Divine Mother promise to be at our side through it all. It is only God who is with us from our first breath to our last; it is only God who will be with us on our astral journey in between lives here on earth and for all time.

Even on a human level, a great master has a thin veil of ignorance in order to play his or her role on earth.

See possible problems in the light of God. He is working out His will through us, His willing instrument—in fact, it is for this purpose that we have taken incarnation and there is no place we would rather be than here and now— because this is where He has placed us.

I am His—heart, mind, and soul—He is my Beloved, my infinite Beloved.

I stand on the threshold of Eternity.

To stand on the threshold of eternity and sing His song is all there is.

Although Jesus is the Master of the ages, still he demanded nothing for himself. He did not need to be worshipped, he did not even want word to go out of his healings; rather, he instructed those who experienced his grace to worship their mutual Heavenly Father.

—∞∞—

Not speaking is not real silence. Only by stilling the body and the mind do we beget true stillness. Then, inner stillness is born in the heart: a place of deep connection with the Infinite Divine that is the firm foundation for the oneness with God.

—∞∞—

To be established in inner stillness brings about the extraordinary state of oneness.

—∞∞—

In deepened meditation we have a growing awareness of the great "I AM" within, beyond the body, even superior to the mind and the individual soul.

—∞∞—

Full realization comes when every part of you knows God and there are no dark corners of opposition left. Then you can no longer stall or crash, for every part of you knows the truth, and you will never have even the slightest desire to trade that freedom for anything else—it simply makes no sense to you to do so, on any level.

—∞∞—

God is living His life in your form, and He loves the life He creates, for at each stage of creation, He pronounces, "It is Good." To truly know this, you must, of course, be in harmony with His will. As you thus harmonize, you will find that you are truly made up of the fabric of God, and it is so woven into your being that you and He are inseparable—even in the midst of organized-chaos.

⸻

To know and follow our true purpose is the greatest adventure, for the soul's ultimate purpose leads us to our spiritual Home—God-realization.

⸻

Really, when it comes to it, there is no such thing as brother or sister, mother or father; there is only one Being who is perfect, pure, and all-pervading—all expressions are of this one Spirit. Therefore, I am really only knowing something about my Self, for there is no other.

⸻

When going beyond dualities realm, and our Divine Friend is our very Self, the "conversation" continues, as He is with us as divine thoughts moving through our mind, and sacred emotions flow through our heart. So, whether in duality or beyond, God is the one constant that takes us through all stages of life and is ever our well-wisher.

Let us deepen our conversation with Him now and we will discover that our Friend of friends is waiting for us this very moment.

The concept of time is a strange one. Circumstances can make a desperate moment seem forever, and in happier situations, time speeds up. In some chapters and books, life can go by almost without knowing that time is making us flow downstream, gobbling up years, and other times are condensed—all compact, and densely-lived. Whether the plasticity of time appears slow or fast, we have but one absolute measurement that is our polestar in life to help us keep our bearings and make us know who and what we are—to be consciously aware of our true Self.

"May Christ be risen in you today." This is an ancient orthodox Easter morning Christian greeting. This implicit message is that the Christ story is everyone's hidden potential—the Christ Principle is part and parcel of the human being's makeup.

Let us visualize our Self as the highest and best core part of us; it operates through our ego-self, and in turn, exercises will power through the mind and body.

A spiritually tuned will is sensitively aligned to the Self or God's will.

God delights in expressing Himself as unique, divine personalities.

———

I asked God, after a very full day of experiences, "Is there anything else You have for me now?"

The response I got was immediate and affected me to the core of my soul. It began with a tremendously powerful inner sound of Aum. Following on the heels of that sound, I found myself in an enormous Cathedral of Light, extending far into the distance in front of me. There were massive columns of Light on either side of the Cathedral which only added to the light already shinning from this marvelous structure.

Then with tremendous speed, but with no sense of motion, I moved toward the front of the Cathedral. At the front where the wall behind the altar would normally be, I saw a tunnel of Light. As I continued to move forward, I entered that tunnel, and as I progressed through the tunnel, I saw a brilliant five-pointed star in the center; the star grew larger as I moved forward.

Without hesitation, I entered the star and then merged into it. I had left the Cathedral far behind me. My body identification was with this vast realm of Light that the star had become. My body was now the Light of the star, and the Light of the star spread all over the earth, and it extended out into vast, unlimited space. I remained merged in that expansive Light for some time, experiencing unparalleled freedom, peace, and expansion.

Later, when I had returned to consciousness of this body, I felt directed to write of this tremendous experience. This revelation is a wonderful meditation on the inner birth of Christ Consciousness. Through inner attunement, you may feel its truth and power.

The Light of Christ Consciousness has redemptive power, and as souls around this world join together in this Light, the world is reborn into higher consciousness.

—∞—

How can we remain in a shadow existence when that is not who we are? Realize there is so much more to us. Let us demand our birthright, proclaim our freedom, and manifest all that we are in truth. This is the task for which we have come and it waits for us to step into the Divine Image and Likeness of who, and what, we truly are.

—∞—

A state of Self-realization is not something to achieve, such as making something new, rather it is something you have ever been, only are unaware of it.

—∞—

In Wordless Prayer, you first feel yourself lifted into Divine Consciousness—His bliss, His upliftment, His power; then, God turns your attention upon any particular person, situation, or part of the world, or for that matter, the whole world itself. Then, you experience all of the power, bliss, and upliftment you are feeling merge into the focus of your prayer.

Time and space collapse; even barriers we call death offers no resistance; the freedom and pervasiveness of God-consciousness are the means for quickening the subject of your prayers with all that you have in Divine Union. No words are needed, only the powerful awareness of all that God is.

Union, yoga with God, is our natural state, and our spiritual practice brings to conscious awareness this pre-existent fact.

On the way up to this exalted state of awareness, we stand with our feet in two worlds: one foot in material existence, the other in the awareness of God's Presence. It is in this sometimes tenuous, in-between state that we must demonstrate the utmost integrity—not slide into forgetfulness of Divine awareness.

We live in this world, we fully participate in it, and we share our concern for its wellbeing, yet we never forget the core of who and what we are in God. That must come first, the world, second.

Do not ignore the call to dive deeper, soar higher; do not live with regret for a single day wasted. We are not here to lead a half-dead zombie life, sleepwalking through old habits that no longer serve us. Rather, we are here to live a dynamic life filled with love, light, and wisdom—a God-realized life.

Divinity is born. Sacredness is awakened in us. What greater promise can bc fulfilled?

⎯⎯ ᘓᘐᘔ ⎯⎯

When we enter our inner Temple, know that we sit on holy ground and all eternity is before us.

Great revelations search us out: are we receptive to the Truth that will transform us and the world?

⎯⎯ ᘓᘐᘔ ⎯⎯

TRUST

The rhythm of time marches forward with a feeling of flow between individual and universal, not so much as distinct, but like an ocean flows into a bay, and the bay flows into the ocean, and where they meet, is both ocean and bay blended together. The thought enters, "This moment, this time is perfect."

———◦◦◦———

This feeling of connection with God, grace, comfort, and inner assurance is what makes all the difference. When you feel connection with God, you may shed tears, feel sadness, even the twist of pain in the heart in grief and yet your soul is not overcome with it. Along with pain will come comfort, peace, and even joy.

There are ways to proceed through grief that do not bind you to the ignorance of separation from God: When you open your heart to the great Comforter you will have a balm to heal the wound of grief. When you stand as an observer on the banks of the river and see/feel your grief flowing through your own heart, flowing out in front of you and letting it go, then you may experience the pain and loss that is mighty, but it is endurable, and you will have peace.

When you let go of anger, disappointment, and pain about a loss, and you do not let it separate you from your Creator, then, with time, the very same thoughts of loss

that created pain in the beginning will transform into feelings of love and gratitude.

—⊶⊷—

Surely, you have been given tasks to do in this world, and
there are times that, like a bridge bearing a large load, you
can creak and groan. However, even when life seems to
be straining you, even then, you may feel true joy. The
secret is to remain identified with the Self. Step back
from the challenge, observe the movie of this life from
the projectionist booth with God at your side. "Fine joke
Ram! Look where you have put me now. Surely You mean
well, You, must guide me and show me the way through."

—⊶⊷—

Knowing that to God, all of His angels, and the spiritual
masters, there are no secrets, there is no place to hide,
and everything is known, then only a fool can believe no
one will know. Jesus said it most graphically when he said:
"That, which you think you do in secret will be shouted
from the rooftops!" (Luke 12:3, adapted).

—⊶⊷—

Even with this material prosperity, what is profoundly
clear to me is that happiness begins within. If every material thing was suddenly gone and all I had was God, I truly
know that in Him I have everything!

—⊶⊷—

I know in every cell of my being that God-experience is the source of every happiness, and it is separation from Him that makes suffering. My soul melts and merges with Him, then He re-animates me to serve Him in all forms, and it is all His play. This—I know.

⸻

Faith in the Master Forger: faith that He knows exactly what He is doing will give you the endurance to remain in the crucible and take all that He metes out to you. Trust and faith are alloys in your being that allow the transformation to go on with the best results.

Surely, your trust and faith will be tested, but that is part of the strengthening and clarifying process you have to undergo. Do not fear, enter the crucible knowing full well that you are ever under the loving care and watchful eye of the Master Forger.

⸻

We learn to strike when He prompts us to strike, and to reside in Him in pure trust when there is nothing for us to take action upon. Like the wise blacksmith, he knows that to strike upon iron when it is not yet up to temperature is uselessly spent energy. When the iron glows the right color of red, then it is time to strike the iron to give it the shape wanted.

So too, when listening to God, He prompts us to strike when it will do the maximum good. Anxiousness will have us flailing about uselessly, wearing ourselves out with what turns out to be destructive actions because we are not attuning ourselves to Him.

How do I go about deciding what to do next? The first thing I do is I go inside and commune with God. I still the mind, turn the whole matter over to Him. I feel peace and quiet in the inner Presence; that is my starting point.

I know with a certainty that God is in charge of this whole play. There is a mighty purpose behind all that He does, and I am content to play my role as He so chooses.

Can you grow taller by anxious thought? We may need a shot of adrenaline now and then to accomplish some task, but constant anxiety is such an awful waste. Let us learn to have God-experience here, now.

You may have fear concerning some experience coming your way. Fear disconnects you from God; it builds fear upon fear and will dominate your life; it makes you think of the worst scenarios and you feel helplessly caught. The fact that you are made in the likeness and image of pure transcendent God-consciousness is completely obliterated by the fog of fear.

Surrender to God means you use your powerful will to focus your mind upon God, not the images of fear. You affirm that God is at the core of your being; it is His Light, courage, strength, mirthful-joy, and love that act as angel's wings to lift you above the clouds of doubt and enclosing fear.

There is not a single thing that occurs in this wide world that is beyond the knowledge and care of the Creator.

We work to lift this world closer to God. True, there are powerful forces of darkness in operation at this time. However, there are also wonderful souls stiving to bring in the Light, for themselves and for this world.

We can spend an enormous amount of energy worrying about some outcome, but in truth, all the worry in the world does not change what is going to be. Worry also produces a negative result as stress to our physical and mental health. With the reasoning mind in charge, it can decide on proper action, or to remain in a restful, alert state. The emotional mind drives us to action, but the actions are usually not for the good. Also, the emotional mind acts as static on the mental radio which interferes with the intuition of the superconscious mind. So not only does the emotional mind have a negative effect on the body and mind, but it also makes it impossible to hear the still, small voice of God within. The reasoning mind can be employed to become calm in meditation, a perfect receiver for superconscious inspiration and guidance. Therefore, the reasoning mind must be in charge.

I live in a human body that has limitations, and He makes me know that I also live in Him and that has no limitations—and in that, I am also content. In the end, He will decide, moment to moment, what His will is for me—I am content.

—◦◦◦◦—

Be always attentive to God's Presence, you can never guess when or where it will take you up.

—◦◦◦◦—

Beauty can grow in the most terrible conditions.

—◦◦◦◦—

A product of realizing God is to naturally live in the moment. The past is a river whose waters have flowed by and returned to the ocean—something to be remembered, but is now given back to God.

The future is in the Infinite's hands, and if there are concerns for what may come, then faith, trust, and reliance upon the Supreme brings peace in the moment.

—◦◦◦◦—

Faith in God means that we keep our mind on Him; we think of His qualities of being all-powerful, all-conscious, everywhere present, all love, bliss, and joy. We know that He is above us, beside us, everywhere about us, and securely found within us.

He is guiding us and the events around us that lead us into His tremendous kingdom of heaven. Our faith brings us into harmony with Him, and we realize, in greater and greater measure, the truth of who and what He is, and of who and what we are. Faith such as this obliterates fear and makes us do all things in full confidence that He is ever with us, and we are ever in Him.

—◦◦◦◦—

Faith in God means that we trust, trust that whatever He brings us is exactly right for us. We have faith in His guidance and wisdom and know that He is with us as well-wisher, friend, and comforter.

It does not mean that waters are always smooth and easy; but really, we do love an adventure. With God, the good ending of the adventure is always assured, but it is still an adventure.

———

Many of the great warriors down through time had absolute faith in the fact that, if it is their time to die, nothing can stop it, and if not their time, nothing can bring death; so, either way, they could charge fearlessly into battle.

———

The one thing that we, as devotees and aspirants may depend upon, is that through our oneness with Him, God will be ever-present with us. We may feel His peace, love, joy, inner direction, wisdom-thoughts, comfort—all that is His.

For reasons known and unknown, we may have certain things we must go through, but in our faithfulness, God will never abandon nor forsake us. This is His promise.

———

While walking amongst desert sage, we are in wonder at the sudden gust of wind as well as the surge of bliss that delivers us into a birth of new consciousness. This type of mystery is knowable in the sense that you can have direct experience of it. However, in nature, as in Spirit, there will always be that which is unknowable—mind cannot know it all; it must simply be experienced.

In this mystery of heaven and of earth, we may be at ease, for it is all held in perfection by the one living God.

———

It is not a formula type thing—simply leave your job and expect God to take care of you; rather, it is living the attitude of seva (service to Him) and knowing that as you do so, whether you are the owner of a company or an employee, He will look after all your needs. It takes a one-hundred-percent participation for this law of God to be fully enacted. When you do, then God joyfully gets busy organizing every detail of your life for your and the world's highest good.

———

As I walk these battlefields near General Washington's field headquarters close to Yorktown (Virginia, USA), I am sure there were those on both sides who performed right action to the best of their ability. However, I, and many many millions, have been the great beneficiaries of the courage shown by those colonists who believed in the ideals of freedom, desired to have a representative government and a guarantee of individual rights.

I honor those who lived up to the highest light of their times and take inspiration that I, and all of us, should be courageous in being examples manifesting the great Light of God within and without in whatever way He directs.

I do think that this country's (United States of America) origins have spiritual inspiration behind them. When we look at the number of despotic tyrannies that crowd our history books, it is a reminder what a unique moment in time it was when guarantees of freedom were stated and put into law.

Today, it seems there is a rush to highlight any blemish under the guise of truth, but fact, without context, is not truth when it is used simply as a bludgeon; there are universal principles.

Traditions around the world speak of a deepening relationship with God—a marriage with God. This feeling for God as your all and all, your Beloved, is both dual in nature: of being lover and beloved; it also holds out a promise for the complete merging of two who become one.

Not all will awaken to this transformed life in this lifetime, but there are those destined to live in Him and shed His qualities to all the earth. As one or two awaken, so that quickens the lives of others, and one or two awaken over there, then there, and on and on, it spreads as the world is lifted into greater heights. When a significant minority transform—not that large of a percentage, actually—the transformation will spread all over this earth.

Suddenly, it will not be about money, power, and fame, but about recognizing the Light in one another and in the world itself. Even though the world may be no great support to those living a spiritual life at this present time, there is no greater opportunity to be in the vanguard of what is to come—to help lead the way through your own example. For I can tell you from my own experience, there is no greater way to live this life than to be in the grip of God.

─────

Faith runs through every part of your life, and each day you can assess your progress in the development of perfect faith.

With faith, you have peace, inner assurance, and a true knowing that God is guiding and protecting you. Faith is a true basis for your spiritual life.

─────

My friends, be not afraid. Each cross is perfectly fitted to its wearer. Yours is perfect for you, even as mine has been for me. It is Love that sees you through; it is Love that makes all possible. Go boldly forward, knowing that all is in His sweet hands, shaping your soul into His likeness and image with the utmost care. For you are not different from He; He cares for you even as you love the Infinite Beloved.

It is love that gives to love—and the rose blooms in the desert.

─────

No two lives are identical, so do not compare yourself to any other, for that would deny the uniqueness of how God chooses to be in you as a co-creator with Him.

So, at any time you are feeling too cramped in your living space, feeling the pressure of life, and that you are too small for the shoes you are wearing, then, instantly, recall who and what you truly are—a child of the infinite—as such, you expand to be larger than the problems and challenges you face; you walk amongst the stars and vast resources are streaming to you in order for you to live your life exactly as it has been ordered from above.

―❦―

"Do not be afraid," He whispers. For all is well, all is He.

―❦―

When souls become realized, more than ever their consciousness may be known wherever a keen desire and love attracts them.

―❦―

Oh, to be present to God with no attachments, no artificial limits—no fear of infinite expansion, nor to being taken into the minute world of subatomic matter—to go anywhere God takes you, without fear or desire, is perfect freedom. The active ego-mind is transformed into the witness to what is; and all that is, is Divine in origin.

―❦―

As God showed me while I was giving a talk, the fierce face of Kali, with her accompanying symbols, is the outer form only—the outer fierceness symbolizes this world. Just as the image of Kali is terrible, tongue dripping blood, holding a sword, skulls hung about, so too can this world be terrifying with wars, famines, pestilence, illness, suffering of so many varieties.

Yet, mystics from time immemorial tell us that the world is God. The word is a sacred expression of its Creator. One can wonder how anyone can say that when there is so much hardship? It is because the mystic dives deeper and comes up with a magnificent pearl of wisdom.

The spiritual master sees not merely the outer fierceness of the world but perceives the Divine Presence underlying all creation. To the penetrating mind, the beautiful Divine Mother reveals Herself behind the ugly image of Kali and the suffering of the world.

Everyone loves a good story, whether told orally, in a book, or a film. And the best stories entail the hero's journey. Such a story portrays the hero being drawn to a course of action, often taking it reluctantly, an action in which he or she must leave all that is known and familiar and set out to accomplish a noble and selfless goal. The nature of such a story is such that it entails the risk of death, or actual death and then an eventual return, or rebirth, and the attainment of something new, better, and more expansive—so pervasive and enduring are such stories that they belong to the collective unconscious.

—∞∞∞—

Information coming from this inner communion varies according to Divine Will: from specific information to a general sense of being, from past life influences to what may occur in coming times. No curiosity or delving into more than what is given is triggered by such inner communion but a very simple trust that whatever comes to me is what is needed in the moment. Physical proximity is not a requirement.

Spirit is a time-and-space annihilation. Communing through Spirit operates through a substratum present in all creation.

—∞∞∞—

Start the collaboration with your Beloved—sincerity is all that is required. It is we who have kept the door closed, so we must open it with we honest approach to Him. Simply, we must open our heart to our Heavenly Father, receive the warm comfort of our Divine Mother, play with our beloved Friend, talk over our troubles with our wise Counselor.

Let us walk hand in hand in times of peace, so that when trials shriek, we need only reach out, and there we will find our most sacred Beloved.

—∞∞∞—

One of the most intimate ways to be with our Maker is to be in conversation with Him throughout our days and nights. Union with God presents a variety of ways to be in relationship with our deepest Soul connection.

Since it is quite human to talk as a means to share information, and to grow closer by sharing our deepest thoughts and feelings, why would we not be conversing with our Heavenly Father/Divine Mother in just that way?

———

There is something here in these ancient towers of stone, a multibillion-year-old earth that speaks to the listening soul. It tells of ages gone and ages yet to come. It vibrates a deep sympathy to a quiet soul. It teaches us to measure time in a completely different manner than humans normally do, and it hints at a quiet understanding that all is well. How quickly a human life must seem to these ancient sentinels, how fleeting are our concerns and worries.

These ancient ones teach us patience and perspective. They demonstrate that great beauty rises from their midst, and then crumbles back into its source once again—in all these comings and goings that span hundreds of thousands of years, these stalwart ones' whisper, "All is well, all is well."

———

God, even now, sends you all you need in the present and for what is to come.

———

The more we attune to God, the more we know it is God who thinks, breathes, and acts through us.

In God, every difference need not separate us in Spirit. Rather, first, find the unity operating beneath the great diversity of creation. Being established in this unity found in God-consciousness allows for the unfoldment of harmonious differences. Each one may hold firm opinions, yet there is a recognition that it is all God's play, and that God enjoys His play.

God within you chooses your level of interest and involvement in the rough-and-tumble world of politics, but whatever He chooses for you, you are always mindful that this is theater; underneath, all are actors playing parts. By not losing contact with God, you do not get lost in the play.

With stillness there is no fear—there is only perfect trust and reliance upon God alone.

This world is God's inscrutable play, and He is in charge of it all, and He works for the highest good in all He does.

Feeling that God and Gurus are with you each step of the way brings strength and a knowledge that all is going according to the Divine Plan.

Time in meditation anchors us to the true Self—then we can go out into this world and do all as His faithful servant.

Let us paint a new picture of ourselves so that when we meet a challenge, we automatically access our connection to God: "Lord, what would You have me do? You are the creator of the entire universe and You have the answers I need. You have the supply that is required. I am Your child and You must see to it that I have all I need to succeed."

Then, feel that from behind the body, there is a flow of intelligence and wisdom coming as creative, uplifting thoughts. Life-force is flowing providing unlimited energy and health-inducing radiance. There is a pipeline of abundance flowing from unknown and delightful sources.

Do not waste your time and energy on nervousness, which has never accomplished a good and noble act; rather, know God as the ultimate resource, comfort, and guide. The quality of your life will change in remarkable ways. There is no greater or more effective way to live your life than to be God's instrument and live with full faith and confidence in His Presence.

Let us join in that superior Spirit that no harm can touch, and no separation can ever reach.

When it comes from God, it will be automatically be for the highest good of all, though not all may welcome what God has given.

⸺⧯⸺

Expand into the heavenly realm of which there are count-less mansions of experience. You may sit in simple silence with your Friend, enjoying the fullness of the moment, or He may be a volcano of inner awakening, yet you are unafraid and trusting.

All is He, all is He.

⸺⧯⸺

Conclusion

Yogacharya David, Sarnath, N. India, 1998.

Prayer
Prayer for World Enlightenment
O Infinite Light of God
You are the indwelling Presence
Within all creation
Both animate and inanimate.

We pray to You
For the eradication of
All conflicts and fights
Both within and without.

We charge you with the responsibility of
Leading all Humankind,
Both individually and collectively,
To live in harmony and with their highest Light.

O Beloved indwelling Presence
You see to it
That dharma—right action
Is established on earth.

And through right behavior
Corresponding to natural and Spiritual law
Peace will reign supreme
And all Humankind will be uplifted
To your highest Light.

Om Peace Bliss Amen[10]

OM TAT SAT AUM

---

10   Yogacharya David. (2021). *Climbing the Sacred Mountain: Poems and Prayers of a Western Yogi* (p. 211).

References

Arnold, Edwin, Sir. (1905). *The Song Celestial or Bhagavad Gita*. London, England: Dryden House.

Hickenbottom, Yogacharya David. (2023). *Climbing the Sacred Mountain: Poems and Prayers of a Western Yogi*. *(2021)*. Camano Island, WA.: The Cross and the Lotus Publishing.

Hickenbottom, Yogacharya David. (2023). *Living a Spiritually Rich Life: Discourses Volume One: 2013–2014*. Camano Island, WA.: The Cross and the Lotus Publishing.

Hickenbottom, Yogacharya David. (2023). *Re-Union of Soul and Spirit: Discourses Volume Two: 2015*. Camano Island, WA.: The Cross and the Lotus Publishing.

Hickenbottom, Yogacharya David. (2023). *A True New Birth: Discourses Volume Three: 2016*. Camano Island, WA.: The Cross and the Lotus Publishing.

Hickenbottom, Yogacharya David. (2023). *Gateway to the Infinite: Discourses Volume Four: 2017*. Camano Island, WA.: The Cross and the Lotus Publishing.

Hickenbottom, Yogacharya David. (2023). *Standing on the Threshold of Eternity: Discourses Volume Five*. Camano Island, WA.: The Cross and the Lotus Publishing.

Hickenbottom, Yogacharya David. (2024). *Writing in the Book of Life: Discourses Volume Six*. Camano Island, WA.: The Cross and the Lotus Publishing.

Swami Sri Yukteswar. (1949/1963/1990). *The Holy Science.* Los Angeles, California: Self-Realization Fellowship.

Bible References

King James Bible Online:
https//www.kingjamesbibleonline.org

Website References

Yogacharya David's original discourse reference:
www.crossandlotus.com

Anandashram reference: www.anandashram.org

Thomas Paine reference: https://www.goodreads.com/
quotes/36115-tyranny-like-hell-is-not-easily-conquered-
yet-we-have

Image Attribution

All images are used courtesy of the David and Carla Hickenbottom portfolio. Photos were taken by David and Carla Hickenbottom or gifted with permission by friends, family, and devotees. Attribution for images from these sources has not been included here.

Acknowledgments

Yogacharya David has a unique ability to share spiritual teachings and soul-enhancing reflections in a most accessible manner—he can reach us in our day-to-day ways of being as we strive to live a purposeful life. He guides us, and even as he laughs at himself, he still seriously advocates for a wake-up process.

It is a privilege to form what we call Team-David, a small dedicated team of aspirants who willingly devote time and expertise to ensuring that Yogacharya David's legacy of teachings reaches those who long for a deeper, broader, disciplined-yet-freeing approach to life's journey.

Carla Hickenbottom, David's wife and senior disciple, has been a major support throughout the preparation and publication process. Her loving oversight and her diligence as director of The Cross and The Lotus Publishing support us each step of the way.

Rebecca Harvey has been a major ongoing link to data collection and historical document searches. She seems to know just where to find more information on most everything we need. Her keen eye also provides an astute read that catches the forever-escaping grammatical challenges. Charmie Gilcrease received 200 pages of quotes from me and lovingly took a year to theme them, brilliantly choosing to place Yogacharya David's words where she felt they best fit. It is a gift of Grace to have such a fine team working to prepare and publish Yogacharya David's legacy of teachings.

Jan Westendorp of Kato Design and Photo brings her artistic and professional book-design expertise forward when working on our manuscripts. She provides us with elegant page layouts and image refinement support, and in so many other ways, she has helped us create a beautiful series of six volumes of *Discourses*, two volumes of *Quotes* plus four other publications, totaling twelve to date.

Of note, some of the quotes have minor grammar or word-placement changes in order to present a teaching in a succinct quote format.

Team-David feels that Yogacharya David would be delighted to know that his unique writings and teachings are available in book form for all who seek a deeper, sacred understanding of the human condition.

About the Author

Yogacharya David Hickenbottom (1954–2019) met his guru Yogacharya Mother Hamilton, a disciple of Paramhansa Yogananda, when he was a youth of 20. Mother Hamilton bestowed the Yogacharya title to David before she left her body in 1991.

The great Kriya Yoga lineage of India that came through Jesus, Babaji, Lahiri Mahasaya, and Sri Yukteswar to Yogananda, and then to Mother Hamilton, provides pathways to: an appreciation of, and a faith in, the everyday sacred, an understanding of higher dimensional wisdom, an integral intuitive knowing of spiritual truths, and the vibratory realms that permeate all that is, was, and will be.

Yogacharya David says: "An inner pain brought me to the path most unwillingly, and this inner pain kept me on the path. I put my shoulder to the wheel." He faced the crux of the spiritual dilemma—how to shift from the ego-driven lower or smaller human nature to a larger and luminous existence, intuitively attuned to our deeper and broader—vast—spiritual nature, thereby discovering the Living Truth. With this intense striving for Truth and Bliss, and with his Guru's Grace, David was carried through many years of Mystical Crucifixion spiritual experiences. His year in silence (2000–2001) established an inner state of stillness that never left him—and finally led him to his full Self-realization.

Also by Yogacharya David

Hickenbottom, Yogacharya David. (2024). *Resurrect the Listening Heart: Quotes Volume One.* Camano Island, WA.: The Cross and the Lotus Publishing.

Hickenbottom, Yogacharya David. (2025). *Seek the Sacred Code of the Universe: Quotes Volume Two.* Camano Island, WA.: The Cross and the Lotus Publishing.

2013–2019 Discourses Series: published 2023–2024.

- *Discourses—Volume One: 2013–14: Living a Spiritually Rich Life*

- *Discourses—Volume Two: 2015: Re-Union of Soul and Spirit*

- *Discourses—Volume Three: 2016: A True New Birth*

- *Discourses—Volume Four: 2017: Gateway to the Infinite*

- *Discourses—Volume Five: 2018: Standing on the Threshold of Eternity*

- *Discourses—Volume Six: 2019: Writing in the Book of Life*

Hickenbottom, Yogacharya David. (2022). *Touching the Supreme Spirit*: Infinite Calendar. Camano Island, WA.: The Cross and The Lotus Publishing.

Hickenbottom, Yogacharya David. (2022). *Silence: Entering the Cosmic Sea of Consciousness.* Camano Island, WA.: The Cross and The Lotus Publishing.

Hickenbottom, Yogacharya David. (2022). *Notes to Sadhakas.* Camano Island, WA.: The Cross and The Lotus Publishing.

Hickenbottom, Yogacharya David. (2021). *Climbing the Sacred Mountain: Poems and Prayers of a Western Yogi.* Camano Island, WA.: The Cross and The Lotus Publishing.

Hickenbottom, Yogacharya David. (2019). *My Spiritual India.* Camano Island, WA.: The Cross and The Lotus Publishing.

. . . and more coming
please visit www.crossandlotus.com